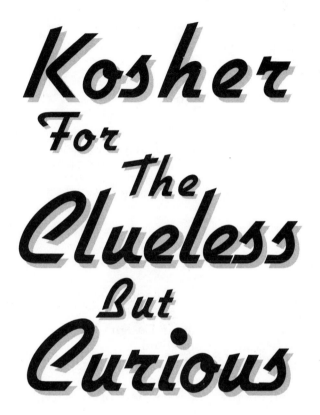

Kosher For The Clueless But Curious

Kosher for the Clueless but Curious
by Shimon Apisdorf

Copyright © 2005 Shimon Apisdorf

Leviathan Press
25 Hooks Lane, Suite 202
Baltimore, Maryland 21208
(410) 653-0300
http://www.leviathanpress.com

ISBN 1-881927-31-8

PRINTED IN THE UNITED STATES OF AMERICA

Cookbook insert by Elizabeth Gething Graphic Design
Food photos © 2005 Marty Katz Photography
Icons and jacket design by Staiman Design
Page layout by Teichman Design Studio
Author photo © 2005 ER Studios

Select recipes and photos appear courtesy of ArtScroll/Mesorah
Publications, Ltd.
1-800-MESORAH (637-6724) http://www.artscroll.com
    Kosher by Design © 2003 Mesorah Publications, Ltd.
    Kosher by Design Entertains © 2005 Mesorah Publications, Ltd.
    Kosher by Design: Kids in the Kitchen © 2005 Mesorah Publications, Ltd.

Distributed to the trade by Biblio Distribution
    (800) 462-6420   http://www.bibliodistribution.com

Distributed to Judaica booksellers by Judaica Press
    (800) 972-6201   http://www.judaicapress.com

All books from Leviathan Press are available at bulk order discounts for
educational, promotional, and fundraising purposes. For information call
(800) 538-4284.

STAR-K KOSHER CERTIFICATION

For countless generations, one of the hallmarks of Jewish life was the "kosher kitchen." Just a generation or two ago, many Jews, regardless of how involved they were in Jewish activities, instinctively shied away from pork and shellfish. With time, however, kosher began to recede into the background of Jewish consciousness. Yet, in recent decades, there has been a resurgence of interest in kosher. Year after year, as more and more people discover the beauty and meaning of their heritage, the kosher renaissance grows stronger and stronger.

The Star-K, as one of the major international kosher certification agencies, has seen this revival of interest manifest itself as a surge in demand for kosher products. Today, there are virtually no culinary interests and delights that can't be had by the kosher consumer.

In addition to our role as a certification agency, the Star-K has also spearheaded a number educational initiatives designed to assist the ever-growing market of kosher consumers. *Kosher for the Clueless but Curious* is one such effort. We are proud to have commissioned a volume that we know will inform and inspire the lives of so many. In this book, Shimon Apisdorf not only presents the laws of *kashrut* in a clear, accessible manner, but allows the reader to understand the deeper spiritual dimension of *kashrut* as well. He has distilled the wisdom of our sages in an engaging, humorous, and enlightening fashion.

On behalf of the Star-K, we sincerely hope that this book will help quench your thirst for Jewish spirituality as well as help you satisfy your appetite for food that is as kosher as it is delicious.

Dr. Avrom Pollak, President
November, 2005

ACKNOWLEDGEMENTS

Jennifer Stein, Eric and Yoni Sunshine, Yitta Baila, Mr. Schatel, Hillel Soclof, Ariella Blas (our favorite commis), Chaim, Shaindl, Nesanel, and Gavi Stein, those wonderful guys at Judaica Press, Fred Glick, Margie Pensak, Ava Gottlieb, Patty Prince, James Ross, Renee Benjamin, Rachel Dadusc, Susannah Greenberg, Rabbi Shlomo Porter, Sam Glaser, Nachum Segal, Paul "Lamed Vav" Goldstein, Aryeh Goetz, Rabbi Bentzi Epstein, Bruce Green, Rabbi Tzvi Holland, Rabbi and Mrs. Yigal and Rifka Segal, Bayla Neuwirth, Irv Naiman, Reb Itchie, Eagle Eye, Stella, Albert, Zoe, Eli, Binyomin, Rachel, Yosef Chaim Dovid, Linda Forman, Rabbi Butler and everyone at Afikim, Avrumi and Tobey—Mazel Tov, our spectacular neighbors, the Efrons, and Dovi Leventhal!

Fred: please call.

APPRECIATION

Dr. Paul Volosov. A man of character, integrity, and vision. Thank you for the vote of confidence. Dr. and Mrs. Michael and Linda Elman, for use of their beautiful kitchen. Gedaliah Zlotowitz, for assistance above and beyond the call of duty. Jennifer, for everything, including the Seven Mile aisle-by-aisle list. Susie Fishbein, Scott Sunshine, Rabbi Menachem Goldberger, and Jen. Shoshana Teichman, for too many late nights at the computer. Elizabeth Gething, for working with your heart. Sharon Goldinger, for putting up with a rebellious author. Ditzah, for all your help on the big day. Yitzie, for saving the book. Baruch, for finally going to sleep. E.R., for Sunday mornings at the Lloyd Street Shul. Miriam, for every time "I'll be home in ten minutes" turned into three hours. Bill "marching band" Hackney, the funniest graphics guy on the planet. Rabbi Asher Resnick, a true friend. Rabbi Michel Twerski. Rabbi Noah Weinberg, Rosh Hayeshiva and source of inspiration.

SPECIAL THANKS

Bubby and Papa Apisdorf. For your love, encouragement, and so much more. Mom, thanks for teaching me how to chop liver.

Grandma and Grandpa Rothenburg. We all love you very much.

Esther Rivka, Ditzah Leah, Yitzchak Ben Zion, and Baruch Chananya. You are each a delightful blessing, and lots of fun too.

Miriam. The source of light in our home and in my life. To walk with you is a treasure. To laugh with you is a wonder. To smile with you is what I pray we do forever. One day, with one of those ideas, we are going to hit it really, really, big.

Hakadosh Baruch Hu, source of all blessing.
L'shana Ha'bah B'Yerusholayim.

Kosher For The Clueless But Curious

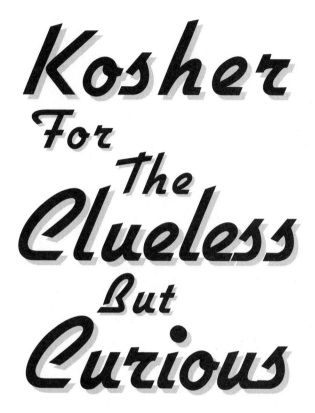

SHIMON APISDORF

leviathan press™

wisdom for the mind, inspiration for the soul™

CONTENTS

Here you will meet our cast of clueless icons. These friendly icons appear throughout the book and each has its own personality and its own unique story to tell.

And you thought kosher was only about meat, milk, and borscht. This chapter explores the lesser-known side of kosher. This is where you begin to understand kosher as a discipline brimming with poignant insights and one that is designed to promote Jewish spirituality.

A topical listing of short, informative, and easy-to-understand explanations of everything from pareve, pork, and *glatt*, to fins, scales, and *cholov* Yisroel.

Chapter 7

The Best of the Rest of the Pantry   191

These five mini-chapters are six to nine pages in length. Okay, so one of them is longer: whaddya' going to do about it?

Introduction
Green Eggs and Clam

A number of years ago, I was working with Tracey Hayes, the convention manager at a Hyatt hotel in Columbus, Ohio. We were planning a breakfast reception for a group of fifty people. But this wasn't just any old breakfast reception; this was a kosher breakfast reception. What's more, this was the first time Tracey had ever organized a kosher event. She was very accommodating, and after about an hour all the pieces were in place. As our meeting was about to end, a serious look came over Tracey's face and her voice dipped to a reverent whisper.

"Do you mind if I ask you something?" she said.

I assured her that she could feel at ease asking whatever she wanted to. To make sure that I understood the seriousness of her question and to highlight just how sensitive she wanted to be to my feelings, Tracey came out from behind her desk, sat down in the chair next to mine, and struggled to get the words out.

"Please don't be offended, but could you explain what kosher is all about? I've never done a kosher event before, and I'm really curious."

This book is an answer to that question.

Kosher just might be the most well-known facet of Judaism. Jews and non-Jews alike, even if they know nothing about

Judaism, in all likelihood have heard about kosher. After all, kosher-style hot dogs are sold in delicatessens and restaurants everywhere, many grocery stores have kosher aisles, kosher is one of the special meal options for airline travelers, a number of Major League Baseball stadiums now have kosher stands, and I recently heard a popular radio talk show host respond to a caller's suggestion regarding a government policy by saying, "I'm not sure that would be kosher," and he clearly assumed that everyone in radioland would know what he meant by that.

At the same time, though the word kosher has become so well-known that it's now a part of the vernacular, its true meaning remains highly misunderstood. If you ask the average person what kosher means, the answers you will most likely hear are, "Kosher means a rabbi blessed the food," "Kosher means the food is very clean and sanitary," "Kosher means no pork," and "Kosher is part of the ancient Jewish health code." In fact, kosher is none of these.

If I were to sum up kosher in one sentence, I would say the following: **"Kosher is a comprehensive dietary discipline designed to promote Jewish spirituality."** So there you have it; while almost everyone thinks that kosher has everything to do with the body—hot dogs, pickles, cleanliness, and health codes—in fact, what it is actually all about is the soul. And this brings us to a fundamental concept that is essential to understanding not only kosher but almost everything else about Judaism.

THE BODY AND SOUL OF JUDAISM

Have you ever sat on a deserted beach when the sun was setting over the horizon, when a breeze was blowing and gentle waves were rolling ashore, when evening was beginning to wrest control of the sky, and asked yourself, "What's it all about?"

Deep within each and every one of us is a longing—a restless yearning to feel connected to something infinitely deeper, infinitely more profound than the familiar cadence of the daily grind we call "life." It's not that there is anything wrong with life; it's just that we feel there has to be something more, something that transcends everything else.

This longing, this tug that seems to emanate from the deepest part of our being, is the rumbling of our soul. The Jewish understanding of human beings is that we are at once fundamentally earthly as well as intrinsically spiritual beings. We are creatures of the flesh, with urges and appetites and desires. And at the very same instance, we are creatures of the spirit, with urges to soar and appetites for meaning and desires for encounters with spirituality.

To the Jewish mind, the difference between people and angels lies in one basic fact: people have bodies and angels don't. The difference between people and animals goes beyond the fact that we are clever enough to put animals in zoos as opposed to being turned into tourist attractions ourselves. The seminal distinction is that people have souls, and therefore spiritual lives, and animals don't.

And God created the human in His image. And God formed the human from the dust of the earth and He breathed into his nostrils the soul of life.

Gen. 1:27, 2:7

The Hebrew word for "soul," *neshama*, also means "breath." When God formed the human from the dust of the earth, this was the body. When God breathed into the nostrils of man, He joined a soul to the body He had already formed. It was the fusion of these disparate elements, body and soul, that formed the complete human being. Further, it is this unique fusion of body and soul into one holistic being that is the basis for all of

Jewish life, from beautiful Shabbat prayers right down to the sandwiches we eat and the cappuccinos we drink.

> *It is inherent in nonkosher food that its consumption*
> *closes one's heart to spirituality.*
>
> Babylonian Talmud

Junk food is dissonant with the body, while whole foods nourish the body. Nonkosher food is dissonant with the soul, while kosher food facilitates the soul's ability to express itself through the life of the body. When it comes to living a full, deep, and inspired spiritual life, a spiritually *Jewish* life, kosher is a necessary ingredient. In and of itself, kosher food is not sufficient to create a spiritual life, but without it, a Jew is simply incapable of accessing his or her fullest spiritual potential.

IT TASTES GOOD, AND IT'S GOOD FOR YOUR SOUL TOO

It's possible that at one time kosher foods may have had health benefits or kosher kitchens may have rated higher on the sanitary scale, but today that is no longer the case. If there is a health dividend to kosher, that is merely a fringe benefit. The essence of kosher today is what it always was: the spiritual diet of the Jew. If, however, one is looking for other tangible fringe benefits, the one timeless benefit is the role that kosher plays in the cultural, social cohesiveness of the Jewish people. A common Jewish diet makes for a common Jewish bond, and this is a benefit that always will tie Jews together.

When all is said and done, this is a book about food, kosher food. And, just as cuisine is a window into the spirit of any people or culture, the same is true for the Jewish people. Judaism is an all-encompassing way of life, a grand holistic system of spirituality. In some ways, kosher is a world unto itself—a huge chunk of a classical, religious Jewish life—but it is also more.

Just as a tree can't be fully understood independent of the ecosystem of which it is a part, the same is true for kosher: it just can't be fully appreciated independent of the life system known as Judaism. For this reason, you will find in this book just about everything you ever wanted to know about kosher, and lots and lots about Judaism as well.

So, while you may have thought that you purchased a book about kosher, you also got a book about Judaism, spirituality, and life. For Jews, after all, what is life, spirituality, and religion without a good kosher meal?

Oh, the Icons You Will Meet

Five icons appear throughout the book, each with its own personality and each with its own little story to tell. Meet the icons:

Myths & Facts • There are a lot of myths floating around about kosher. Whenever this icon appears, it means that one of those myths is about to be clarified. Each "myth & fact" moves you one step closer to becoming the neighborhood kosher expert.

• This icon introduces many of the basic kosher laws and provides brief explanations about how they are applied in the real world.

● Most people who think about kosher think about food, food, and more food. In reality, while kosher is about food, it's not all about food. Kosher is very much about the soul. This icon presents short insights into the deeper realm of kosher.

● When it comes to the practical application of kosher laws, there are instances where there is a range of scholarly rabbinic opinion on precisely how to apply certain laws. This can be confusing, particularly for the novice. This icon alerts you to prominent examples of such laws and encourages you to seek the guidance of a rabbi to help you navigate your way.

● There is a lot of confusion in the world about whether or not certain foods are kosher. This icon briefly explains why some foods that people may think are kosher are not.

● **Important Notice:** Each icon in this book stands on its own and is not integral to the main text of the book. As you encounter each icon, you can either take a short break from the primary text and read the icon or you can ignore the icon completely and just keep reading the body of the book. The choice is yours.

Chapter 1
Some Soul for the Food

The understanding of kosher as a discipline designed to promote Jewish spirituality means that woven into the structure of this dietary system are numerous elements that inspire and nurture the soul. It also means that beyond food, Judaism relates to eating generally as a potentially deep, spiritual activity. This topic is divided into two parts and presented in two chapters that touch on some of the deeper dimensions of kosher food as well as "kosher" eating.

The first part begins here. The second part begins on page 83.

FROM WHOLE FOODS TO HOLY FOODS

No grocery store chain in the world is growing at the rate of Whole Foods Market. In 2003, with just 150 stores, Whole Foods made $30 million more in profits than Food Lion, even though Food Lion had 800 more stores.[1] Safeway, Kroger, Albertson's, you name it, they are all losing ground to Whole Foods, and the reason, clearly, is that Whole Foods is not as much about food as it is about life. The Whole Foods Market phenomenon is testimony to the fact that our society has embraced the notion that there are clear, fundamental, and demonstrable links between food and emotions, food and energy, food and mood, food and peak performance, food and well-being, and food and happiness. Once upon a time, people went grocery shopping so that they could satisfy their hunger with foods they enjoyed. Today, they go shopping for foods that can help them become the people they want to be.

Researchers in England have demonstrated that dietary adjustments can significantly reduce violent behavior in inmates. Want 37 percent less fighting, guard assaulting, and hostage taking in your prison? Just make sure your inmates have a diet rich in vitamins, minerals, and essential fatty acids.[2] In Japan, Canada, and Puerto Rico, researchers have uncovered links between diet and stress-related diseases, brain function, anxiety, and depression.[3] And the links between food and general wellness don't stop there.

Is anyone you know a sugar addict? If you answered yes, and if this person exhibits symptoms such as wild mood swings, severe crankiness, fatigue, irritability, and periodic sobbing, then hang on, because help is on the way. It's called SugarShock.com. (No kidding.) And let's not forget the soda-and-junk-food-stuffed vending machines that practically line the halls of our schools. Talk to just about any educator and you'll be told that half of the problems with kids in school are directly linked to what's in those machines. In the spring of 2005, Governor Arnold Schwarzenegger announced, "We in California this year are introducing legislation that would ban all sales of junk food in the schools."

We live in a society that takes the relationship between food and the well-being of the total person, not just the body, very seriously.

For over three millennia, Judaism has also considered the relationship between food and the complete person to be a very serious matter. In Jewish thought, kosher is linked to sanctity and spirituality, to the kind of discipline that is the hallmark of integrity and morality, and to character. Together with Shabbat, there is little that rivals kosher food when it comes to transforming the life of a Jewish person into a deeply *Jewish* life. Then, when we expand our horizons and look at kosher in the broader context of the Jewish understanding of food and eating in general, it becomes clear that Judaism firmly believes that food is not only essential for sustaining life, but for elevating the quality and deepening the meaning of the lives we lead.

Myths & Facts

Myth: Kosher is sort of like Jewish magic. The rabbi waves his wand and says a few words, and presto, the food is kosher.

Fact: If kosher is hocus-pocus, then the U.S. Food and Drug Administration is one big Las Vegas show. In fact, ensuring that food is kosher is a sophisticated matter that incorporates chemistry, biology, technology, and spirituality all in one.

If Judaism is about anything, it's about a people with a unique mission to have a revolutionary impact on the world. (Either you will have to trust me on that or you can check out my book *Judaism in a Nutshell: God*.) The Jewish people are called to be nothing less than a "holy nation" and have a mandate to be "a light unto the nations." Food plays an essential role in that mandate. Interestingly, John Mackey, the founder and CEO of Whole Foods Market, seems to understand the hidden potential that food represents. "Whole Foods is not a business for a clique or for the elite. We wanted the philosophy of the stores to spread throughout the culture. We wanted to change the world."

In the following essays, we will explore a number of highly important, though often overlooked, dimensions of kosher and the Jewish understanding of food.

[I] KOSHER CIVILIZATION

Most of our essential physical needs function in an involuntary fashion. We don't consciously choose to breathe, we don't will our hearts when to beat, we don't think about our eyes needing to blink; these necessities just take care of themselves. Eating is different. We absolutely must eat to survive and to function properly, but eating doesn't take care of itself. Eating is a necessity that involves regular awareness and an ongoing need to make conscious choices. This dual nature of eating, that it is both an inescapable necessity as well as an act over which we are capable of exercising great control, is one of the defining factors that separates people from animals. It is also one of the reasons why kosher is so central to Jewish life.

Consider this: The one word that every child absolutely hates to hear from her parents is "no." Yet, we parents are aware that one of our fundamental responsibilities is to teach our children that there is such a thing in life as "no." Far more important than listening to us is that they learn to say no for themselves.

If you think about it, it's pretty clear that the basis for civilization is self-control. With it, civilized society stands a chance. Without self-control, no matter how many laws are in place, we are doomed to a world run amok. A world populated by people without self-control and self-restraint will quickly devolve into an ugly, brutal, self-centered, and self-indulgent world—not the kind of world any of us wants our children to grow up in.

I did not grow up in a kosher home, but my wife and I do keep kosher. I still remember when our first child, who was then about four, asked my mother if a cookie she was being offered was kosher. My mother couldn't get over the realization that a four-year-old could have that kind of self-control and not just pop the cookie in her mouth first and ask questions later. I have to admit, I was pleasantly surprised myself.

Having the ability to control her urge for a cookie says a lot about a child. I believe that it also says a lot about Judaism that once that child is sure her cookie is kosher, the Jewish attitude is "Go ahead, enjoy your cookie."

In Judaism, the ability to be able to sometimes say yes and sometimes say no to one's most basic appetites is not only the sine qua non for a civil society but also for a holy one.

[II] THE BODY AND SOUL OF LAMB CHOPS

Animals with claws are not kosher. Any animal that nourishes itself by tearing other animals to pieces and eating them is simply not a part of the Jewish diet. Bear, mountain lion, hyena—forget it, they're not kosher. Cow and lamb are fine. For an animal to be kosher, it must have split hooves. Split hooves are quite suitable for standing around on, but they are pretty useless as hunting weapons. In addition to not being hunters, animals must be herbivores to be kosher. Not only must kosher animals be herbivores, but they must also be ruminants, meaning they must have a four-chambered stomach that allows them to redigest their food. Rabbi Samson Raphael Hirsch was a great scholar, a major figure in Jewish philosophy, and a statesman who lived and taught in Germany in the mid-1800s. In his writings about kosher animals, he observed the following:

> In Jewish law, all vegetables are permitted for food, without discrimination. Next in order of desirability as human food

would come those animals that are herbivorous and therefore nearer the vegetable world. [Kosher animals] show little vivacity and passion, temperate instincts and little [aggressively] powerful animal activity. Among animals that chew the cud, only those that have cloven hoofs have four stomachs. After the food consumed has passed through two stomachs, it is driven up the gullet again, and chewed for a second time, and then led through the other two stomachs one after the other. These animals spend a great deal of time in the absorption of food that may be termed the vegetative activity of animals. In contrast, carnivorous animals have short intestines and little time is wasted on the more passive and plant-like activity of digesting the food.

Rabbi Hirsch, *Horeb*

Judaism understands the human being as a blend of spiritual and physical, body and soul. The two, in essence, are in a partnership, though the soul is viewed as the senior partner. It is the job of the soul to create and articulate each person's mission statement, to identify meaningful goals, and to show the way in the pursuit of those goals. The role of the body is to implement the soul's plans for a spiritual, moral, meaningful life, not to make plans of its own. If there is any truth to the notions that we are what we eat and that the foods we ingest can indeed have a profound impact on our psyche, as well as our physique, then what Rabbi Hirsch said has profound implications. The more our diet consists of foods that are rich in "animalistic" qualities, the more our own bodies may be inspired to strike out in an aggressive manner that will be at odds with the gentler, more refined inclinations of the soul. In Rabbi Hirsch's words, "Anything that brings it [the body] nearer to the animal sphere, robs it of its primary function to be the intermediary between the soul of man and the outside world."

ROCK-'N'-ROLL, KOSHER CHICKENS, AND HUNTING

One of the most popular rock-'n'-roll guitarists of all time is Ted Nugent. In addition to being a legendary performer, he is also a best-selling author and a hunting enthusiast. Not only is Nugent a big-time hunter who leads all sorts of safaris, he is also an advocate of eating what you kill. In his latest book, *Kill It and Grill It*, he states that his family hasn't bought meat from a grocery store since 1969.

In that spirit, he penned and proclaimed the following on his web site:

I hunt because I am a hunter. A primal urge boils throughout my entire being, driving me to flex my ultimate independence through self-sufficiency and rugged individualism. Killing the ultimate fresh, pure, natural health food for my family is job one for this American husband and father. Before an arrow is loosed or a cartridge ignited, the spirit of the hunt feeds the inner being the most incendiary fuel known to man. I crave it all. I am CraveMan.

No vampires allowed

Blood is not kosher and must therefore be drained from all meats. This removal involves a two-step process. First the meat is rinsed and soaked, and then coarse salt is applied to draw out the blood. Not long ago, people did this on their own at home. Today, virtually all meats sold by kosher butchers have already been drained of all blood.

According to Nachmanides, one of the greatest scholars of the medieval period—a period that was exceptionally rich with scholars whose writings remain classics to this day—some of the underlying principles inherent in kosher food seemed to be aimed directly at the heart of the kind of passion that drives Ted Nugent to hunt, kill, and eat his prey again and again and again:

> An insight into why certain birds are forbidden is because their consumption has the effect of making a person more prone to brutality. It could be that this is also true of forbidden animals. There are no carnivorous animals that chew their cud and have split hooves. All other animals hunt for their food. And, this violent characteristic can be transferred to someone who eats such animals.
>
> Commentary of Nachmanides (Ramban), Leviticus 11:13

Somehow, I don't think Nachmanides would be surprised to know that Ted Nugent's nickname is the Motor City Mad Man or that in an interview on CNN, he spoke about his daughter Sasha who shot her first buck when she was seven years old. When asked if seeing the animal dressed traumatized her, Nugent replied, "Traumatized? She gutted the bugger. She loved it. She knows where food comes from, and it's the purest form of food known to man. So she takes that deep into her heart."[4]

I'm sure Ted Nugent is a good father and that Sasha is a sweet girl. Nonetheless, "kill it and grill it" is not what the Torah wants our children or us absorbing into our precious hearts and souls.

[III] MUNDANE GREATNESS

Have you ever wondered why God arranged for Moses, the greatest leader in all of Jewish history, to have his first real job as a shepherd and not as a stockbroker or brain surgeon? The answer is simple, and it goes to the heart of what true greatness is all about.

A man is not elevated to greatness without first being tested with seemingly petty matters.

Medrash

Our sages tell us that Moses, like Abraham before him, was a shepherd for a reason. It was a test, and the test was this: would Moses, son-in-law of the wealthy and influential Jethro, allow his father-in-law's sheep to nibble from the neighbors' grass, or would he take his flock on some circuitous route to wild fields where he could be sure the sheep wouldn't be eating—and thus stealing—grasses that didn't belong to Jethro?

Think about it. God could have tested Moses by having him slay a three-headed dragon or an evil Cyclops. He could have tested his devotion, mettle, and commitment by having him make an epic journey to rescue an innocent damsel in distress. He could have tested Moses's character by having him tempted by a bribe the size of a king's ransom, but He didn't. Instead, all God wanted to know was, "Does this guy have the integrity to work harder, week after week and month after month, than others might think necessary, just to make sure that no one else is robbed of a few patches of grass?"

And guess what? Moses passed the test. The willingness of Moses to make this seemingly trivial effort demonstrated to God that Moses was truly the man for the job—the ultimate job.

Now, do you think you can guess where the Torah itself makes this point? If you guessed that this idea is brought out in the context of the laws related to kosher slaughtering, then you hit the nail on the head. (And you probably also peeked at the answer.) Let's now take a look at a few lines from the Torah along with the commentary of Rashi. (Rashi lived in France in the eleventh century. He was a wine merchant and scholar. His writings on the Torah and the Talmud are the most widely studied of all the classical commentaries.)

First, the Torah:

For I am God who elevated you [when I took you] out of the
land of Egypt for the purpose of being your God; therefore, you
should be holy because I am holy. This is the teaching regarding
the animal, the bird, every living creature that swarms in the
water and every creature that creeps on the ground. Distinguish
between the impure and the pure, between the animal that it is
permissible to eat and the animal that may not be eaten.

Lev. 11:45–47

And now, Rashi:

When one examines these verses in light of what the Torah
teaches about permissible and impermissible animals, a
question immediately arises. The question is this: Elsewhere, the
Torah explicitly teaches about which animals are permissible
and which aren't, and exactly how to "distinguish" between the
two. This being the case, why does the Torah again need to speak
about a "distinction" between permissible and impermissible
animals? Isn't this a redundancy in the text?

Rashi addresses this question and says the following:

Of course we already know which animals are kosher and which
are not. However, these verses are actually only referring to
kosher animals and are addressing the possible imperfections in
the slaughtering process that can render an otherwise
permissible animal, impermissible. And, these imperfections can
be so minute that they are only detectable by a well-trained eye.

With Rashi's comments in mind, if we go back and reread the
verses from the Torah, what we find is a sublimely grand
concept packaged together with hair-splitting minutiae. In the
first verse, the Torah speaks about the great event of the Exodus
and God's calling of the Jewish people to live on a lofty spiritual
plane, and in the next verse the Torah warns us to be careful
about tiny imperfections that could render an otherwise kosher
cow unfit for Jewish consumption.

A powerful idea is revealed in this juxtaposition: true
greatness is to be found in the countless small, unnoticed, and

Vitamins and Supplements

I'd Better Ask

Kosher vitamins, herbal and homeopathic remedies, and supplements are widely available at your grocer, health food store, and on the Web. Nonkosher vitamins are also widely available, but you don't want those. For guidance on when it is okay to take vitamins or remedies with nonkosher ingredients, it's best to consult a rabbi.

unapplauded acts that together make up the great tapestry of life. It's true that greatness can be found in someone who is willing to die for a just and meaningful cause, but an even more profound kind of greatness can be found in someone who lives for a just and meaningful cause, day in and day out, in all that he or she does, no matter how petty or mundane the task may seem to be. Which brings us to the kosher kitchen.

What in the world could possibly be more mundane, more pedestrian, than preparing, serving, and eating a meal and cleaning up afterward? Yet it is precisely there, in the kosher kitchen, that the roots of Jewish greatness lie. Jewish history is replete with people who made the ultimate sacrifice rather than deny their belief in God and Judaism, and every one of those people is a hero. At the same time, Jewish history is even more awash in countless people who demonstrated their utter devotion to God and Judaism, day after day, by being extra careful about precisely how their meat was slaughtered, what ingredients they used in their soup, which spoon they used to stir the pot, which bowl they allowed the soup to be eaten from, and which dishes were washed with which after dinner. Can you imagine someone being put on a sugar-free diet by his or her doctor—for life—and never once even sneaking a sip of Coke? Jews who keep kosher look not only at what they eat but also at everything associated with what they eat as one big spiritual diet from God, and they never sneak a bite of bacon—ever. This is because in the mundanity of the kitchen we find the deep sanctity and uplifting spirit of a relationship with God just as much as we find it in the sanctuary of a synagogue.

It just may be that the ability of so many Jews to express their heroic commitment to Judaism is rooted in their daily willingness to make hundreds of small, unheroic commitments to God.

Chapter 2
All That Kosher Stuff: A Handy-Dandy Kosher Glossary

Kosher is like a planet in the solar system of Judaism. There is a lot more to Judaism than kosher, yet it is a world unto itself—a world with its own laws, concepts, principles, and vocabulary. This glossary will acquaint you with the vocabulary of kosher so that you can smoothly navigate this book, and converse like a pro the next time you are with people who keep kosher or find yourself in a kosher restaurant or store.

The glossary is divided into four sections: Meat and Milk, and Keeping Kosher; The Kosher Kitchen and Kosher Consumer; Israeli Food Products; and Common Kosher Terms.

[I] MEAT AND MILK, AND KEEPING KOSHER

Blood
The Torah forbids eating the blood of animals and birds. Fish blood is permitted to be eaten. The most common method for removing blood from meat is by salting the meat (see Kosher

Salt), though it can also be removed by broiling the meat. An issue of blood spots in raw eggs also exists. (See Eggs.)

Cholov Yisroel

Literally "Jewish milk," *cholov* Yisroel is milk whose production was supervised by a Jew from the time of the actual milking until the conclusion of the production process. The purpose of this supervision is to ensure that no milk from a nonkosher animal is mixed in with the kosher milk.

Historically (and even today in many countries around the world), it was common practice for dairy farmers to mix various kinds of milk.

Today in the United States, Canada, and other countries where strict government regulations outlaw the use of any milk other than cow's milk in commercial plants, many rabbinic authorities are of the opinion that it is not necessary to have a Jew present. Nonetheless, many people prefer to "go the extra mile" and only consume *cholov* Yisroel and other dairy products produced with *cholov* Yisroel.

Eggs

Eggs from kosher birds are kosher. Eggs from nonkosher birds are not kosher. In addition to the requirement that eggs come from kosher birds, another issue is the potential presence of an embryo in a fertilized egg. Embryos are not kosher. The presence of a blood spot in a raw egg may be a sign of fertilization. For this reason, raw eggs must be checked for blood spots, and if a spot is found, the custom is to discard the egg.

Fleishig

Fleishig is a Yiddish word meaning "meaty." The word is used to identify food that can't be consumed with dairy foods. It goes without saying that meat is fleishig, but sometimes a food can be fleishig without containing actual pieces of meat. For instance, carrots removed from a pot of beef stew are fleishig and cannot be eaten at a dairy meal. Cookware, dishes, and cutlery used exclusively for meat are also referred to as being fleishig.

The term fleishig is also used in the following way: a person who had a meat sandwich for lunch and is then offered a piece of cheesecake may politely demur by saying, "Thank you, but I'm fleishig."

Glatt Kosher

Glatt is a Yiddish word that means "smooth." (The Hebrew term is *chalak*.) It refers to a procedure that takes place after a kosher animal has been properly slaughtered. For an animal to be kosher, it cannot have any illness or serious injury at the time it is slaughtered. To ensure that an animal did not have any serious internal defects, a postslaughter inspection of major organs is performed. For example, the lung is checked for tears or lesions. If any kind of puncture or lesion is found that clearly indicates the lung had been torn, then the animal is not kosher.

The issue of *glatt* arises when a lesion is found that may or may not indicate a tear in the lung itself. In such a case, the lesion is carefully removed and the lung is inflated and submerged in water. Any bubbling indicates a tear, and the animal is deemed not kosher. If no bubbling occurs, then the animal is kosher, even though a lesion was present and the lung is not *glatt* (smooth). This means that even after a kosher animal has been properly slaughtered, it remains to be determined if the meat from that animal is (1) not kosher due to a defect such as a tear on the lung, (2) kosher but not *glatt* kosher because of the presence of a nonserious lesion, (3) *glatt* kosher because the lung was perfectly smooth and lesion free.

In addition to the technical meaning of the word *glatt*, the term "*glatt* kosher" is frequently used in a colloquial sense to mean "very kosher" or "extra kosher." From the vantage point of Jewish law, however, only meat can have the status of being either non-*glatt* kosher or *glatt* kosher. Fish, soup, salad, pizza, and all other foods are simply kosher or not.

Insects

The vast majority of insects are not kosher. Today, the practice is not to eat any insects at all. A number of common vegetables often contain insects and must be carefully examined before they can be eaten. These include lettuce, broccoli, raspberries, and strawberries. A rabbi or friend who keeps kosher can teach you how to properly check vegetables for insects.

Every time we are about to eat, we have an opportunity to use the physical world for a spiritual purpose. If, before eating, we reflect on the notion that the purpose of eating is to enable us to have the health and strength to do good and to live a spiritually centered life, then we elevate food into something spiritual.

Kosher for Passover

Foods that may be kosher at all other times are not necessarily "Kosher for Passover" because of a unique prohibition of not eating any leavened or fermented grain products throughout the week of Passover. This means that foods such as cookies, crackers, cereals, beer, breads, and pastries are no-nos on Passover. The same is true of foods that contain even small amounts of grain products. So, while it's obvious that your average granola bar won't be kosher for Passover—because the main ingredients are grains—it's not self-evident that ketchup, which may contain small amounts of ingredients derived from grain, is also off-limits for Passover.

Thus, the ubiquitous "Kosher for Passover" labeling means that a particular food or food product has been produced in accordance not only with the general rules of kosher food production but with the unique rules that apply to foods on Passover.

Kosher Salt

Kosher salt is salt that contains no milk or meat ingredients. (Just kidding. Wanted to see if you were paying attention.)

Kosher salt is a coarser-than-usual kind of salt that is used to kasher raw meat. Because of the prohibition against eating blood, kosher meats must be drained of all blood prior to cooking them. One of the methods for extracting blood from raw meat is to cover the meat with salt, which draws the blood to the surface. Not long ago, it was common for kosher butchers to sell meat that had not been "kashered," meaning the blood still needed to be extracted. People would buy kosher salt for use at home to draw out the blood.

Milchig

Milchig is a Yiddish word meaning "dairy" or "milky." It is very common to hear silverware, restaurants, and food products referred to as being either fleishig, meat, or milchig, dairy.

Milk and Meat

Milk and meat are the two general categories of food that can never be cooked or eaten together. Separately, of course, many dairy and meat items are perfectly kosher. This means that even two food items that are perfectly kosher on their own, become perfectly *treif* when mixed together. (See *Treif*.)

Pareve

Pareve is a term meaning "neutral." Pareve foods are neither meat nor dairy and can be eaten with either. Examples are fruits, vegetables, most breads, most beverages, spices, rice, pasta, tofu, Slurpees, and cotton candy.

Pork
Though pork is no less kosher than snails or squirrel, it has achieved *the* status of the nonkosher food par excellence.

Salting Meat
See Kosher Salt.

Shechita
For the meat of a kosher species to be fit for consumption, it must be slaughtered in a very specific manner. This type of slaughtering is known as *shechita*. The person who does the slaughtering is known as a *shochet*, and every *shochet* must be highly trained and wellversed in all the relevant laws.

Here are some of the basic rules:

- An exceptionally sharp knife must be used so that the animal dies from a clean, almost effortless cut that does not involve any tearing or sawing of the flesh.
- The cut must be made on a certain area of the throat, and both the wind pipe (trachea) and the food pipe (esophagus) must be severed.
- With regard to kosher fowl, it is necessary only that one of those organs be cut.

Traiboring
Traiboring is a process of removing veins and nonkosher fats from kosher meat. Though meat from a kosher animal is perfectly kosher, the blood and certain fats are not. The fats are removed by a butcher after the animal has been slaughtered and before the meat is salted.

Treif
Treif is a generic term meaning "nonkosher." The Hebrew word *treif* literally means "torn" and refers to an animal that died because of a "tear" instead of being properly slaughtered. Despite its narrow, technical meaning, the word *treif* has become

the colloquial catchall for anything that isn't kosher.

Waiting Six Hours

In addition to a prohibition against eating meat and milk together, there is also a prohibition against consuming milk separately immediately after one has eaten meat. However, various rabbinic opinions exist as to how much time must elapse between the consumption of meat and the consumption of milk. The most widespread practice is to wait six hours after eating meat until one consumes milk. Some people, however, do not wait as long. As a general rule, people adopt the practice that was used by their parents or prevalent in their community.

(Note: The same rule does not apply to eating meat after dairy. Though meat and dairy cannot be eaten at the same meal, it is permissible to eat meat immediately after eating dairy foods once one has rinsed one's mouth and had a bite of something pareve to eat. The reasons for this distinction are that the taste of meat lingers in one's mouth far longer than the taste of dairy and that bits of meat tend to get stuck in one's teeth and stay around even after the meat has been eaten.)

MEDICINE

I'd Better Ask

There are a number of potential kashrut problems with medicines. For example, gelatin used for capsules is often made from animals, tablets may contain stearic acid that is derived from animals, and syrups may contain nonkosher flavorings. Nonetheless, Jewish law is extremely sensitive to health issues, and if no kosher medicine is available, one is almost always allowed to take a nonkosher medicine. The Star-K Web site has detailed information about kosher medicine.

[II] THE KOSHER KITCHEN AND KOSHER CONSUMER

Bishul Akum

Bishul akum is a Hebrew term meaning, "cooked by a non-Jew." Some foods are kosher when cooked by a Gentile, and some are not. The term *bishul akum* refers to those foods that are not kosher. (See *Bishul* Yisroel.)

Bishul Yisroel

Bishul Yisroel is a Hebrew term meaning "cooked by a Jew." Before we get to the specifics, let's take a step back and consider Jewish identity.

Sometimes it's easy to forget you are a Jew, and sometimes it's not. As a rule, Judaism views being conspicuously Jewish as a good thing. To be conspicuously Jewish has the dual function of always highlighting and reinforcing the simple existential reality of your Jewish identity while signaling others that you are a Jew and as such represent something unique.

In general, the adherence to kosher food laws frequently makes one conspicuously Jewish, and that's good. In addition to keeping Jews focused on their identity, kosher creates a certain social impetus for a Jew to socialize with Jews. The value of this is that the more Jews socialize with one another, the more likely they are to have Jewish friends, date and marry other Jews, and remain vital members of the Jewish people. This is not meant to be anti-Gentile or racist, just very realistic about the relationship between social events, socializing, and Jewish continuity, and as we know, food is almost always central to socializing. Now the specifics.

The general rule is this: foods that can be eaten raw or that wouldn't normally be served for an important occasion may be eaten even in a cooked state, regardless of who the chef was. Foods that cannot be eaten raw or that would be served at an important occasion must be cooked by a Jew. For an item to be considered *bishul* Yisroel, it is not required that the entire cooking process be carried out by a Jew. Rather, it is sufficient that a Jew at least light the fire that is going to be used for cooking. From that point on, anyone else is free to take over.

Chodosh (and *Yoshon*)
See page 51.

Myths&
Facts

Myth: Kosher means clean.

The following is a true story about someone who was convinced that "kosher means clean": In 2002, a Louisiana oyster distributor began advertising his shellfish as "certified kosher." He had no ill intent whatsoever. The man was exceptionally proud of a process he had developed to purify his oysters. Sure that "kosher" meant clean and pure, he decided to market his mollusks as kosher. Once a local orthodox rabbi informed him that no matter how clean his oysters were, they could never be kosher, he removed the labeling so as not to offend anyone.

Fact: Particularly in the realm of commercial food production, extensive and thorough cleaning needs to take place in order to allow machinery and utensils to be used for kosher foods. Additionally, people who keep kosher are generally very careful to make sure that their utensils are kept clean and never come into contact with anything that isn't kosher. The truth, however, is that while cleaning is an integral part of the koshering process, and while a clean kitchen is certainly conducive to maintaining a kosher home, "cleanliness" is not technically synonymous with "kosher." "Kosher" means "prepared," in the sense that the food has been prepared in accordance with all the laws of kosher.

Hechsher

A *hechsher* is a symbol or certificate that attests to the fact that a food is kosher and has been prepared under the supervision of a qualified kosher supervisor. (See *Mashgiach*.) The term usually refers to a packaged food item or a restaurant and is commonly used as follows: "Is there a hechsher on that candy bar?" "Does that restaurant have a hechsher?" (In Texas it's known as a "heck-sure," as in, "heck, sure, it's kosher!")

Immersion (of Utensils)
See *Toivel*.

Kasher/Kashering

Kashering is the procedure for rendering utensils that have been used with nonkosher foods ready to use with kosher foods. Kashering procedures vary according to the type of utensil, the material from which it is made, and how it was used. For example, a metal spoon used to stir a pot of pork and beans may not be used at a kosher meal. The koshering procedure for this spoon involves three steps:

1. It must be thoroughly cleaned.

2. It cannot be used for twenty-four hours.

3. It must be totally immersed in a kosher pot of boiling water.
   (The practical applications of basic koshering rules are addressed in chapter 5.)

Keeping Kosher

Keeping kosher is a colloquial term commonly used to refer to anyone who is careful about following the laws of kosher. Such a person is referred to as someone who "keeps kosher."

Myths&
Facts

Myth: If the letter *K* is printed on a food package, this means the product is kosher.

Fact: The letter *K* cannot be trademarked and therefore can have more than one meaning on a package. *K* may mean kosher, or it may mean something else altogether.

Kosher Airline Meals

I don't know about you, but I find the variety of foods available on major airlines to be astounding. You want low sodium? No problem. Macrobiotic? Got it. Kosher? Of course!

Kosher airline meals are prepared by a kosher catering service and provided to the airlines. Meals that require heating are double wrapped in foil so that they can be heated in the plane's ovens. To receive a kosher meal, you generally need to place a request twenty-four hours prior to the flight. If you forget to order your meal, don't despair. The little packs of pretzels and peanuts offered by the airlines are almost always kosher (don't forget to check that label), and usually the crew will be happy to provide you with enough nuts to get you from New York to California.

Kosher Bakery

You guessed it. A kosher bakery is a shop where only kosher ingredients are used in baking and only kosher food products are sold. (Tip: Early on Fridays is when kosher bakeries are brimming with delicious fresh challah for *Shabbat*, but make sure you go early in the day to avoid the last-minute rush.)

IT'S THE LAW!

KOSHER COP

The disappearing drop

If a few drops of milk accidentally splashed into a pot of meat sauce, this will probably not make the sauce nonkosher. As long as the ratio of milk to meat is at least sixty to one, the milk is considered to have been totally dissolved and is halachically insignificant. One can eat that meat sauce without any concern that one is eating milk and meat together.

Kosher Butcher Shop

A kosher butcher shop is a store where only kosher meats are prepared and sold.

Kosher Home

A kosher home is a home (apartment, condo, town house, time-share, or tepee) where the occupants observe the laws of kosher and maintain a kosher kitchen.

Kosher "In" and Kosher "Out"

Some people are careful to keep a kosher home but are less strict when it comes to eating in someone else's home or eating in a restaurant. These people keep kosher when they are "in" their homes but not necessarily when they are "out." (According to Jewish law, however, the rules of kashrut apply equally at home, at the office, and at a picnic in the park.)

Kosher Kitchen

A kosher kitchen is a kitchen in a home or restaurant where only kosher foods are prepared and the rules of keeping kosher are carefully adhered to.

Note: Large institutions, such as hospitals and hotels sometimes have separate kosher kitchens that are used only for certain clients or special kosher events.

Kosher outside the House

"Kosher outside the house" is a variation on the theme of "in" and "out." Often, people will measure their degree of commitment to kosher by whether or not they keep kosher outside the house as well as inside.

Kosher Plates and Cookware

Kosher plates are those that are permissible to be eaten, though doing so may result in huge dental costs. Okay, seriously. When someone refers to plates or pots and pans as being "kosher," it means that a certain set of dishware and cookware was designated to be used exclusively for either meat or dairy and not both. This is important because kosher meat cooked in a dairy pot may no longer be kosher. Similarly, pasta with cheese sauce cooked in a pot used to prepare spaghetti and meatballs may also become nonkosher. Certainly, kosher food cooked in a nonkosher pot may also render the food nonkosher.

Note: We all make mistakes. The use of a meat plate or a meat pot for dairy or vice versa does not necessarily render the vessel nonkosher and unfit for future use. If you should slip up and serve a cheese pizza on a meat plate, consult with your rabbi before doing anything drastic.

Kosher Restaurant

Kosher restaurants only prepare and serve kosher food. These restaurants come in two varieties: meat and dairy. Kosher Chinese restaurants are always meat restaurants, kosher pizza shops are dairy, and kosher Italian places can be either meat or dairy restaurants. For a restaurant to be kosher, it should be supervised by a rabbi or recognized kosher certification organization. Most kosher restaurants have certification agreements with a local board of rabbis that has an office dealing specifically with kosher issues.

Kosher Shrimp

There simply is no such critter as a kosher shrimp, but fear not because there is faux kosher shrimp. "Kosher shrimp" is a specialty item made from kosher fish and molded to look like shrimp. So if you ever wondered what shrimp tastes like, or if you would like to indulge an old favorite taste sensation without violating your commitment to keeping kosher, then kosher shrimp is the way to go. By the way, "kosher bacon" is also available.

Kosher Style

You know those knockoff, Gucci look-alike purses you can buy on the streets of New York? Well, that's the same idea as kosher style: it looks kosher, it smells and tastes kosher, but it's not kosher. Kosher style is a marketing idea that appeals to people who think that kosher food is healthier, are attracted by the ethnic appeal of kosher, or are nostalgic for the kind of foods their grandmothers once made.

Kosher Supervision

Kosher supervision is a formal and professional service provided by companies to ensure that commercial food products are prepared in a fashion that meets the requirements of Jewish law. Kosher supervision companies must certify commercial food manufacturers, restaurants, caterers, bakeries, and other entities that want to sell their products to the kosher consumer. The Hebrew term *hashgacha* means "supervision," and any food-related business that is properly supervised is considered to be "under the *hashgacha*" of the supervising company. A kosher consumer who is making an inquiry into whether or not a product or establishment is kosher will ask the question, "What *hashgacha* does this product or business have?"

Mashgiach

A mashgiach is the person who supervises food preparation at a kosher restaurant, event, or manufacturer. As a rule, a mashgiach is employed by a kosher certification company and assigned to work at one or more businesses.

It is common for much of the staff at a kosher establishment to be unfamiliar with the laws of kosher. For this reason, a mashgiach will be on the premises to make sure that the correct procedures and practices are put into place and adhered to. If any questions arise during the cooking or manufacturing process, they are referred to the mashgiach.

Some circumstances require that a mashgiach be on the premises at all times, and others require only periodic visitations. A mashgiach that is always present is known as a *mashgiach t'midi*.

Mevushal (or *Yayin Mevushal*)

Mevushal is the Hebrew word for "cooked." *Yayin mevushal* means "cooked wine."

If you are a progressive, pluralistic-minded kind of person (like most of us these days), then the concept of cooked wine will likely grate on your contemporary sensitivities. But hey, that's the way it goes. Judaism was here long before many of the ideas that are currently in vogue and will be here long after they have become passé. It's my job to tell you the truth about kosher and your job to think about it.

The term *mevushal* is relevant to kosher wines. Though the ingredients in wine may be kosher, the Torah prohibited the drinking of wine manufactured by Gentiles because it was commonly used for pagan religious practices. Additionally, the Talmud prohibited even Jewish wine that was handled by Gentiles after it was opened. Since in antiquity only uncooked or unboiled wines were used in pagan rituals, Jewish law does not restrict wines that are produced and then boiled by Jews.

The Talmud also prohibited the drinking of wine manufactured by Gentiles and of unboiled kosher wine handled by non-Jews after it was opened, even if the wine was not used for ritual purposes. The essence of this prohibition is rooted in the desire to create some kind of minimal social barrier between Jews and non-Jews and thereby minimize the likelihood of intermarriage.

Kosher wine, therefore, usually requires a three-tiered kosher process. First, no nonkosher ingredients are allowed to be used in the wine; second, all critical steps in the process must be done by a Jew; and finally, the wine must go through a boiling process so that both Jews and Gentiles can handle open bottles of wine. A kosher wine that is non-*mevushal* (uncooked) and has been opened, poured, or handled by a non-Jew subsequent to opening is prohibited. For these reasons, the vast majority of kosher wines today go through a boiling process and are labeled *"mevushal."*

Mikvah

A *mikvah* is a small, specially designed pool of water used for various spiritual purposes in Jewish life. Utensils made of metal or glass require immersion in a *mikvah* before they are used for the first time in a Jewish home. This immersion is known as *toiveling*.

Pas Yisroel

Pas Yisroel is bread baked by a Jew.

Two kosher issues are associated with bread and other baked goods. The first, and most obvious, is the ingredients. All ingredients must be kosher. In the case of some breads, the most common nonkosher ingredients are the oils used to grease the baking surface. The second issue is that home-baked bread must, in addition to having kosher ingredients, be baked by a Jew. (See *Bishul* Yisroel for a discussion of this concept). The law that one cannot eat bread baked by a non-Jew applies only to breads baked in private homes and not to commercially baked breads.

It is considered religiously admirable, though certainly not obligatory, for one to eat only *pas* Yisroel baked goods, even if they are commercially manufactured. For this reason, some lines of commercial baked goods, in addition to a certification of being kosher, will bear an indication that they are pas Yisroel.

The laws of kashrut are very deep; deepest of all is that they are God's instructions for life. Nothing can be more profound than for a person to be aware that what he or she is doing is an expression of the will of the Source of all existence. Every time we eat (and that's quite frequently), the laws of kosher give us an opportunity to notice that at the heart of everything in Jewish life is nothing less than the privilege to connect our own will with the will of the Divine. Kosher allows us to to consider the enormous potential we have to bring God into our lives not only in moments of great spiritual inspiration, but into the day-to-day practicalities of life, into our homes, and into our world.

Separate Plates

People who keep kosher have two sets of plates, cookware, and cutlery in their homes: one for meat and one for dairy.

Note: The kosher bachelor who uses only disposable plates does not need to buy separate sets of paper milk plates and meat plates. He can use different plates out of the same package for meat and milk dishes.

Toivel

Toivel is a Hebrew word meaning "dip," as in when one dips utensils in a *mikvah*. (See *Mikvah*.) The word "dip" is a bit misleading because utensils must actually be completely submerged in a *mikvah* and not just dipped.

Vaad and Vaad Hakashrut
See page 54.

Yoshon (and Chodosh)
See page 55.

[III] ISRAELI FOOD PRODUCTS

We live in an absolutely remarkable period of Jewish history. For over two thousand years, Jews everywhere hoped and prayed that one day we would return home to the land of Israel, and today we have. What once seemed to be utterly impossible, that a tiny, scattered, and persecuted people would return to its homeland, is taking place right before our eyes.

One of the opportunities that we were looking forward to during those many centuries of exile was the ability to observe the agriculture-based commandments that are unique to life in Israel. Indeed, one of the many thrills of life in Israel is the ability to observe these commandments. Some of these commandments have kosher implications.

The laws related to these foods, and their practical implications for Israeli produce, are very detailed. Suffice it to say that, while it is very exciting to see Israeli produce and products for sale at your local grocery, you need to be very careful that they have been produced in accordance with the special kosher laws that apply to Israeli agricultural products. In the case of packaged goods, this is fairly easy to do. If the package has kosher certification, then this includes those laws unique to Israel. On the other hand, when it comes to fresh produce that may not be labeled, you need to be sure that the produce is in fact kosher. One way to do this is to call the Star-K hotline at (410) 484-4110. Another way is to ask a knowledgeable rabbi in your area. Finally, you could just move to Israel where such matters are a lot clearer.

Below are very brief explanations of food issues unique to Israel.

Challah
Challah is a "gift" that is given to the Kohanim when there is a Temple in Jerusalem. (See *Trumah and Maaser.*) When one kneads a significant amount of dough (over 2.5 pounds) for baking purposes, a small portion of the dough is removed for the Kohen. Today, instead of the challah dough being given to a Kohen, it is burned. Once challah has been separated from the larger amount of dough, the dough can be baked into bread or other items.

Maaser
See *Trumah* and *Maaser.*

Mehadrin
Mehadrin is a Hebrew word meaning "beautiful." *Mehadrin* is the Israeli version of the colloquial term *glatt kosher*. (See page 33.)

Orlah
Orlah is the term for fruit that grows during the first three years of a tree's growth. The fruit from fruit trees, as well as grapes, cannot be eaten for three years after the trees (or vines) are planted. This law also applies to trees outside Israel. If you plant a fruit tree in your backyard, it is important to consult with

a rabbi regarding how to render the fruit permissible to eat in the fourth year.

Shiviis
Shiviis is the Hebrew word for "seventh year."

Shmittah
The most extraordinary agricultural law in Israel is *shmittah*, the seventh, sabbatical, year. The Torah says that every seven years, agricultural work must stop and the only foods one can eat are those that grow on their own. Today, with the return of a Jewish agricultural industry to Israel, the laws related to *shmitta* are once again very relevant, though an explanation of their application is far beyond the scope of this book.

Tevel
Tevel is the Hebrew term for untithed produce.

Trumah and Maaser
Trumah and *Maaser* are terms for various "gifts" or tithes that apply to Israeli-grown produce. In Israel, one has an obligation to donate certain percentages of one's produce (tithe) to the Kohanim (Kohen) and Leviim (Levi). Although the laws fully apply only when there is a Temple in Israel, the practical implication today is that untithed foods cannot be eaten.

[IV] COMMON KOSHER TERMS

Bishul Akum
See page 38.

Bishul Yisroel
See page 38.

Myths & Facts

Myth: Two people, one eating meat and the other eating dairy, cannot eat at the same table.

Fact: As long as one of the two is using a place mat or something is placed on the table between the two people, they can eat together. These are precautions to make sure that they don't taste from one another's food and end up eating meat and dairy together.

Chew Cud
See Cud.

Chodosh (and *Yoshon*)
Chodosh is the Hebrew word for "new." This refers to wheat that is temporarily nonkosher. (See *Yoshon* for a full explanation.)

Cholov Yisroel
See page 32.

Cud
Ever heard of ABC gum? Cud is the food that is brought up from the first stomach of a ruminant into the mouth where it is chewed again and then redigested. (ABC, by the way, stands for "already been chewed.") The Torah (Lev. 11:3 and Deut. 14:6) says that for an animal to be kosher, it must chew its cud and also have split hooves.

Fins and Scales
Fins are the parts of a fish that help it move and steer through the water. Scales are thin protective plates that cover the

skin of fish. The Torah (Lev. 11:9–10) says that for a fish to be kosher, it must have both fins and scales.

For kosher purposes, "scales" must be able to be scraped from the skin without tearing the flesh. All fish that have "kosher" scales also have fins. The converse is not true.

Fleishig
See page 32.

Glatt Kosher
See page 33.

Hechsher
See page 40.

Kasher / Kashering
See page 40.

Kashrus
Kashrus is the Yiddish version of the Hebrew word *kashrut*.

Kashrut
Kashrut is a Hebrew word that translates as "the whole gamut of stuff related to kosher."

Kosher
"Kosher" literally means prepared. Foods permitted by the Torah and prepared according to Jewish law are kosher.

Kosher Salt
See page 35.

Kosher Slaughtering
See *shechita*, page 36.

Mashgiach
See page 45.

Mehadrin
See page 49.

Mevushal
See page 45.

Milchig
See page 35.

Milk and Meat
See page 35.

Pareve
See page 35.

Pas **Yisroel**
See page 46.

Scales
See Fins and Scales.

Shechita
See page 36.

Shellfish
Shellfish are mollusks and crustaceans. Common examples are lobster, crab, and clam. Shellfish are often thought of as the quintessential treif seafood, though they are no less kosher than other nonkosher fish. Squid, shark, whale, seal, dolphin, porpoise, and seahorse are just as nonkosher as shellfish.

Shochet

A *shochet* is a person who is exceptionally knowledgeable in Talmudic studies, scrupulous in his personal religious life, and expert in the application of the laws of kosher slaughtering. In Jewish communal life, a shochet is regarded as someone of great integrity, despite the fact that he is often seen carrying a very sharp, large knife. Hundreds if not thousands of people may rely on a single shochet for ensuring that their meat is kosher.

Split Hooves

A hoof is the horny covering on the feet of some animals. Horses, for example, have hooves. Leopards and polar bears have paws. The hooves of kosher animals are split, or cloven. The Torah (Lev. 11:3 and Deut. 14:6) says that for an animal to be kosher, it must have both split hooves and chew its cud. (See Cud.)

Traiboring
See page 36.

Treif
See page 36.

Vaad and *Vaad Hakashrut*

The Hebrew word *vaad* means "gathering." In this case it means a gathering of people who are responsible for the proper application of kosher standards. *Vaad* is the colloquial term used for the rabbinic organization that is responsible for kosher standards in a community. Most Jewish communities have their own local *vaad*, or *vaad hakashrut*.

Waiting Six Hours
See page 37.

IT'S THE LAW!

Two sets or one?

A kosher home must have separate sets of dishes, as well as all other utensils, for meat and for dairy. However, the same tablecloths and dishtowels can be used for both dairy and meat as long as they are washed between uses. Of course, in a vegetarian home, one set of dishes is enough.

Yayin Mevushal
See *Mevushal,* page 45.

Yoshon (and *Chodosh*)

Yoshon is a Hebrew word meaning "old." *Yoshon* refers to a type of wheat that is always permissible to eat and is contrasted with *chodosh,* which is temporarily impermissible. This distinction can be a bit confusing, though basically it works like this: For a moment, forget about Rosh Hashanah and January 1 and instead think of Passover as being New Year's. Now imagine that a kosher rule says, "Thou shall not eat harvested wheat until after New Year's." This would mean that if you planted wheat in August and harvested it in January, you could not eat it until after Passover. However, after Passover, you could eat that wheat. Got it? Good.

What we have are two kinds of wheat: one that has yet to cross the magic date of Passover and one that has crossed it. Got it? Good. Now, let's call the wheat that is so young that it hasn't celebrated its first Passover *"new* wheat" and the wheat that has been around long enough to already have a Passover under its belt, "*old* wheat." New wheat, *chodosh*, is temporarily forbidden, and old wheat, *yoshon*, is okay to eat.

Well, guess what? There actually is a prohibition in the Torah that says, "Thou shall not eat harvested wheat until after Passover." Although not in those exact words.

Scholars have a difference of opinion on whether these laws apply only in Israel or also outside the land of Israel. Today, outside Israel, many rabbinic authorities permit the eating of *chodosh*, though many individuals make an extra effort to observe the same practice both in Israel and everywhere else. (To find out more about *chodosh* and *yoshon* and their relationship to Passover, visit Star-K on-line at http://www.star-k.org.)

Chapter 3
"I'll Have the Texas-Style Burger *Without* the Bacon"

Judaism is not an all-or-nothing religion. Judaism fully recognizes that no two people are alike, that each of us lives with a unique set of circumstances, that we all have our own particular challenges, and that what may seem easy to one person can be quite difficult for another. Judaism is also acutely aware of the fact that no one is perfect, that we all make mistakes, and that life is more like a work in progress than a polished masterpiece.

With this in mind, it is important to appreciate that while keeping kosher is clearly the ideal for every Jew, for those who are just getting started, it may be most practical to take a one-step-at-a-time approach. Below you will find an overview of the five stages that people often go through as they begin to keep kosher. Keep in mind, however, that since every individual and every set of circumstances is unique and because no two people approach changes in life the same way, not everything will apply to you. Nonetheless, it is my hope that this chapter will help you traverse the many issues and challenges that often present themselves on the wonderful journey from ham-burgers to hamless-burgers.

THE PROCESS, OR YOU GOTTA START SOMEWHERE

So there you are, sitting at your favorite sushi place with a close friend, someone you trust and can confide in, when you say, "You know, I've been thinking about keeping kosher." Your friend, trying her hardest not to choke on an eel-and-cucumber roll, says, "Are you sure you want to do *that*?"

Beyond her concern that you may never be able to share the joys of sushi again (which isn't true), your friend is literally petrified that you are contemplating becoming one of *them*, as in "You're not going to become all weird and religious, are you?" Well, I'm here to tell you that you can put your friend at ease by telling her, "You know, I don't know if I will ever go that far or not, but I do know that the more I learn about Judaism, the more I want to do something that makes my Jewishness, my spirituality, a tangible part of my everyday life." You can reassure your friend, as well as yourself, that while you have decided to start keeping kosher, you are going to take it one step at a time and that you have no intention of allowing your decision to create any distance between you and the people you care about most, your family and friends.

So now, let's take a look at this one-step-at-a-time process. The chart on page 59 is an abbreviated overview of the process. Following the chart is a detailed description of each step.

STAGE ONE: MAKING THE DECISION

Over two thousand years ago, the Jewish sages articulated a principle called *kol hatchalot kashot*, which means "all beginnings are difficult." The beginning of almost every significant step we take in life comes down to making a decision. Whether it's changing jobs, getting married, moving to a new city, or keeping kosher, the first step is always the fundamental decision to take any step at all.

THE
ONE-STEP-
AT-A-TIME
APPROACH

THE SUMMIT
(6) READY TO KASHER YOUR HOME?
• Read chapter 5.
• Discuss your decision with a rabbi or friend who keeps kosher.
• Go for it.

(5) SWIM LIKE A FISH:
• Begin purchasing only kosher food for your home.
• Eliminate all but your one favorite nonkosher restaurant.
• Seriously consider kashering your kitchen.

(4) LETTING GO:
• Stop eating meat and dairy at the same meal.
• When you are ready, begin waiting an hour or two
after eating meat until eating dairy.
• Begin buying five or six types of products with a kosher symbol.
For example: only purchase tuna, pasta, coffee, ice cream, and
olives with a *hechsher*.

(3) WADING IN:
• Familiarize yourself with a kosher butcher in your city
and the kosher section at your local grocery.
• Eliminate nonkosher meat from your diet. (You can begin only at home
and later stop eating nonkosher meat even away from home.)
• Eliminate nonkosher seafood from your diet.
• Try various pastries at your local kosher bakery.

(2) GETTING YOUR BIG TOE WET:
• Begin by eliminating one nonkosher food item from your diet.
• Start looking for kosher symbols on packaged food items.
• When you are ready, eliminate another nonkosher food item from your diet.

(1) THE DECISION:
You have decided that
• "I am going to experiment with keeping kosher," or
• "I am committed to eventually keeping kosher."

Once you have decided to keep kosher, or at least to begin the process, you have two basic options. You can, and many do, just jump right in. You can go absolute cold turkey on all nonkosher food, stop cooking in your own kitchen until you kasher it, buy a large supply of paper plates and plastic goods in the mean time, stock up on canned tuna, regularly invite yourself over to your "kosher" friends' homes for dinner, and just go for it. Or, as many others do, you can take a more gradual approach, as described in this chapter.

STAGE TWO: GETTING YOUR BIG TOE WET

This is where the gradual, step-by-step approach begins. Good luck, and don't forget to have fun along the way.

1. Eliminate one nonkosher food item from your diet. It's your choice—pepperoni pizza, snails, Philly cheese steak, anything with meat at Taco Bell, nonkosher wine—whatever, but just eliminate something. You can eliminate this item only when you eat at home and later eliminate it even when you are eating elsewhere, or you may choose to completely eliminate it. Again, the choice is yours. This step may seem to be hypocritical—both to yourself and to others—so you will need to remember, and perhaps inform others, that Judaism applauds all efforts on the path of spiritual growth, even seemingly small, incremental efforts.

2. Pick one or two nonkosher items that you regularly buy at the grocery store, and look for an alternative product that is produced under kosher supervision. This will require that you have some familiarity with the various kosher symbols that are printed on food labels. You may need the help of a friend who keeps kosher or a rabbi to help you identify which symbols actually mean "kosher" and which don't.

3. After a month or two, eliminate another food and continue to do so until you are ready to take your next big step.

STAGE THREE: WADING IN

There is no magic formula to the process of beginning to keep kosher. The best advice is not to bite off more than you can chew but at the same time push yourself just a little bit.

Soul Food

Jews have a beautiful tradition that relates how each one of the Hebrew letters asked God if it could be the first letter in the Torah. Eventually, God said yes to the letter *bet*, and so the Torah begins with a *bet*. The reason is because bet is the first letter in the word *bracha*, which means blessing.

The letter *bet* is the second letter in the alphabet and therefore has the numerical value of two. Two is a special number. It represents abundance. A firstborn child is a *b'chor*, a word that also begins with the letter *bet* because the first child is the beginning of abundance; it's with a firstborn that a husband and wife are transformed from a couple to a family.

Before eating food, when we say a *bracha*, a blessing, our consciousness is focused on the abundant goodness, the abundant delight, and the abundant blessing contained in every bite of food. The next time you are about to pop a slice of orange in your mouth, stop for a moment. Focus on the piece of fruit in your hand—on the bright orange, delicately textured peel; the perfectly shaped slice that contains hundreds of tiny packets, each containing a fresh burst of juice and a nice little dose of vitamin C. And the fragrance—it too is marvelous. Put it all together and you have abundance, blessing. So go ahead, when no one is looking, try saying a blessing before you eat, and truly experience the abundance. And then think about the source of *all* abundance.

• •

1. Begin this stage by not eating anything "too *treif.*" For instance, eliminate all pork and shellfish from your diet, as well as any dish where milk and meat are cooked together. This is when you will say goodbye to pepperoni and sausage on your pizza; to shrimp, eel rolls and clambakes; and to the bacon on your Texas-style burger.

2. Next, eliminate all nonkosher meat from your diet. It's at this point that your options in restaurants get seriously limited. Also begin purchasing all your meat either from a kosher butcher, in the kosher frozen meat section of your local grocery, or on-line at Kosher.com or Kosher Bison.com.

STAGE FOUR: LETTING GO

The fourth stage is when things start to get serious. At this point you will begin to feel like you are making a profound change in your life, and the truth is, you are.

1. It's time to take the milk and meat plunge: eliminate milk and meat together, and also refrain from consuming milk and dairy products immediately after eating meat. The

most common custom is to wait six hours after meat until one eats dairy. At this point, however, you may choose to wait an hour or two. Practically speaking, this means that while your veal was kosher and your frozen yogurt is kosher, you will now wait an hour from the time you finish dinner until you have the frozen yogurt for dessert. What may be even tougher than that is waiting an hour to have a cup of coffee with milk after your dinner. This is when you will discover that Tofutti desserts and non-dairy creamers are not as bad as they sound, and neither is black coffee.

It's up to you as to when you will increase the amount of time you wait between milk and meat.

Eel it is. Gefilte it's not.

Kosher fish scales are removable. Eel scales are not. Ipso facto, eel is not kosher.

2. Time to practice *hechsher* hunting. As you know (and if you don't, take a look in the glossary), a *hechsher* is a symbol printed on packaged goods that testifies to the fact that the product was manufactured under the watchful eye of a reliable kosher certification organization. At this stage in your kosher life, begin examining product labels not only to check carb, fat, and chemical contents but also to see if a *hechsher* is printed on the label. Do your best to buy as many products with a *hechsher* as

possible. This will add a whole new dimension to your food shopping experience; have fun.

STAGE FIVE: SWIMMING LIKE A FISH

It may be as little as a few months since you began this journey or as long as a year or two, but whatever the case, you are just about there. You are now poised to fully embrace a whole new chapter in your life, poised to set a standard of spiritual excellence for your children and grandchildren for generations to come, poised to join the ranks of countless Jews throughout the millennia—Maimonides, Yehuda Halevi, Menachem Begin, Joe and Hadassah Lieberman—and poised to annoy your friends and relatives every Thanksgiving from this day forth.

Your final four steps are these:

1. At this point you are going to make one of two statements about your favorite restaurant: either "I guess dinner last Thursday was the last time I'll ever eat at Mama Mia's" or "I'm going to really enjoy myself tonight at Mama Mia's because this is it; after tonight, never again." Regardless of which statement is yours, you have reached the point where *treif* restaurants are a thing of the past.

2. Eat *hechsher*-labeled products only. From this point on, and forever more, if it doesn't have a *hechsher*, you simply can't eat it. (Certain exceptions to this rule, such as for bottled water and sugar, should be discussed with your rabbi.)

3. Allow no more exceptions. Until now, you may have made certain exceptions and looked the other way. They may have been at your parents' or grandparents' home or at the home of a friend who tried very hard to be accommodating but didn't quite get things right. The truth is, settings like these can be the thorniest to

navigate, but from now on there will be no more overlooking kashrut problems. The rule is simple: if it's kosher, you can eat it, and if it's not, you can't. And don't worry—if you handle these situations with common sense and with humor, you will almost always find a way to navigate even the roughest waters.

4. Prepare to kosher your home. The most important "ingredient" in koshering your home is a coach. Your coach is someone who will go through the entire process with you and who will help make sure that you do everything right and that you don't have a nervous breakdown in the process. Your coach should be either a rabbi or a friend who keeps kosher and is very familiar with the rules of kashering. If you choose a friend as your coach, it is advisable to have a rabbi on call should any questions arise during the koshering procedure.

The first practical step you need to take in advance of kashering your home is to buy one or two weeks' worth of disposable dishware and utensils. From the time that you begin to prepare your kitchen until the time you are finished you will be living in a sort of limbo where your home will be no longer *treif* but not yet kosher. Trust me, you will need plenty of paper plates, plastic silverware, hot cups, and all the rest.

If you are ready to make the final jump to kashering your home, then it's time to read the next chapter. Mazel tov and good luck.

FAMILY, FRIENDS, AND OTHER ISSUES

Food is the focal point in a very wide range of social settings. From the business lunch to a weekly visit to grandma, and from birthday parties to Super Bowl parties, there aren't too many social activities where food isn't a prominent feature. For this reason, your personal decision to begin keeping kosher will inevitably become a very public part of your life.

This section provides an overview of what to expect in various kosher-food challenged situations and how to handle them.

OH, THE REACTIONS YOU WILL GET

A whole range of reactions from family and friends is possible when you "become kosher." Some people will have great respect for your decision and even relate to it with a sense of reverential awe. Some will express their own desire to do the same one day and admire you for taking such a brave step. Others will be quite nonchalant—"that's nice" will be the extent of their reaction—and as long as your decision doesn't affect them, they won't care much one way or the other. Some, however, may react with surprise, shock, dismay, and even anger. These are the most challenging, and the ones with whom you will need the greatest patience and understanding.

In most cases, if you do encounter resistance, it will be from those who are closest to you. Parents may feel that you are rejecting the Judaism they raised you with and may take your defection from the ranks of the nonkosher quite personally. You may be accused of making life unnecessarily difficult for others—"You don't really expect us all to go to a kosher restaurant just because you want to, do you?"—or even of causing a rift in the family. In the case of an aunt or grandmother at whose home you have been eating for years, you may be met not only with a generous helping of guilt but even with tears. You can certainly ask people to be as understanding and tolerant of your kosher lifestyle as they would be if you had decided to become a vegetarian, but when it comes to family sensitivities, logic has a way of getting tossed out the window.

I want you to keep one thing in mind. When it comes to dealing with others' less-than-enthusiastic responses to your new kosher lifestyle, they are right: you *are* the problem. *You* are the one who is asking others to accommodate your change, *you* are the one who is making it less convenient for people to socialize with you, and *you* are the one who is now living a far more conspicuously Jewish life. Therefore, since you are the troublemaker, it's incumbent on you to expend as much effort in making this whole kosher thing work for those around you as you expend in making it work for you. This doesn't mean that you need to compromise your commitment in any way, but it does mean that you need to be at least as understanding of others as you expect them to be of you.

EATING AT GRANDMA'S

Tell me, is there a better way to break your grandmother's heart than to tell her you can't eat her food anymore? For that reason alone, you need to meet with your rabbinical coach to figure out what you can do to still eat at Grandma's without betraying your commitment to keeping kosher. If you are living with your parents, then you will certainly need to have this discussion with your coach. Ideally, your parents should also be a part of such a meeting.

The following are some of the topics you need to explore when it comes to eating in a nonkosher home:

- Using a self-cleaning oven
- Doing the food shopping with or for your host
- Using disposable aluminum cookware
- Using your own separate pots and pans
- Kashering a stovetop burner for one-time use
- Kashering a microwave for one-time use
- Eating on paper plates and using plastic cups and silverware
- Boiling water in Grandma's teakettle
- Knowing what mistakes are kosherly fatal and which can be corrected

YOU'RE NOT GOING TO BECOME ONE OF THEM, ARE YOU?

Some people in your life will be convinced that keeping kosher is just one part of a bigger picture and that they may be losing you to the "dark side." They will be concerned that you will no longer accept them as being Jewish, that you will no longer respect their Jewish convictions, and that you will no longer be any fun. What you need to do is find as many ways as possible, in word and in action, to communicate the following: "Our relationship is deeply important to me. It's something I hold dear and would never want to lose. At the same time, my relationship to Judaism is also profoundly important to me; it's a core value that I live my life by. I have no intention of letting go of either you or my personal commitment to keeping kosher or whatever else I do Jewishly. I'm going to do whatever I can to make this all work out, even if sometimes it's rough, and I hope you will do the same."

Finally, these kinds of relationship issues go way beyond the scope of this book, but what you need to know is this: keeping kosher never destroyed a healthy relationship.

THE REAL WORLD

It's one thing to keep kosher in the safe confines of your own home; it's quite another to try to balance the demands of keeping kosher in the context of living and working in a perfectly *treif* world. The following are some general guidelines for common situations. Again, however, I would urge you to consult with your rabbi in terms of the specifics of situations you are dealing with.

THE BUSINESS LUNCH

"Doing lunch" is often as integral to people's business as their computer or telephone. If you are fortunate to live in a city with at least one good kosher restaurant that is reasonably convenient for you and your client to get to, that's great. However, if there are no kosher restaurants or if they are on the other side of town, then what do you do? The answers are simple, and there are four of them:

1. **The boardroom:** Explain to your client that you keep kosher and can't eat in a nonkosher restaurant. (More often than not, the person will respect your religious convictions.) You can then explain that you can have a kosher lunch catered at one of your offices, where you can dine and talk in the boardroom. Of course, this works only if you have access to a kosher caterer. If this isn't feasible, you can order a meal from a restaurant for your client and just bring your own lunch. True, the situation may be a little awkward, but it will probably also lead to some meaningful conversation that you otherwise would not have had. Perhaps that conversation will then lead to a more genuine relationship between you and your client, which will lead to a greater sense of trust and respect, and this will all lead to your landing the biggest sale of your life and eventually being able to retire early with a winter home in West Palm Beach and a condo in Aspen. All because you keep kosher.

2. **"Airline food":** If you need to dine in a nonkosher restaurant, you may have the option of bringing in your own kosher food. Many restaurateurs, particularly at finer restaurants, are familiar with the issue of kosher food. Some will be happy to order a meal for you from a kosher caterer or to allow you to place the order and bring it to the restaurant. The simplest solution is to order a meal that can be served and eaten cold; however, if it is properly wrapped, a meal can be heated even in a nonkosher oven, just like the airlines do it.

3. **Brown-bagging it:** You usually have the option of bringing your own lunch. This may be a bit awkward,

particularly with a new client or colleague, but again, it will probably lead to some good conversation. In this case, it is advisable to contact the restaurant ahead of time to let the staff know what you are planning to do and why.

4. **Fruit and a Coke:** If you are in a nonkosher restaurant and simply can't make arrangements for any kosher food, then your only option is fruit, cold drinks, and perhaps a cup of coffee. You can ask the waiter for an assortment of fresh fruits on a plate and the restaurant's finest glass of Mountain Dew. It's not a problem to use the restaurant's dishes and silverware for your fruit. Of course, another option is just not to eat.

● ●

Every human being is made from the fusion of physical and spiritual, body and soul. The body and soul frequently have competing interests. The soul wants to be kind and helpful, and to live a life of integrity and sanctity. The body, however, is happy to be self-centered, lethargic, and indulgent. Our sages refer to the struggle between the physical and the spiritual as an "inner war." The Hebrew word for war is *milchama*. The root of this word, *lechem*, is also the word for bread.

Many people find themselves at war with food. Sometimes we are able to control our desires and appetites, and sometimes we are vanquished by them. The battle we wage with food is frequently indicative of our deeper inner battle, the battle of the physical and the spiritual. Win the battle with food, and we are well on our way to winning a far more important battle: the battle to live a soul-driven life over one dominated by the body.

• •

DRINKS AFTER WORK (STARBUCKS TOO)

Occasionally after work, some of your coworkers may go to a sports bar around the corner from your office or to a Starbucks to relax and talk. What can you do about eating in these places?

Bar

1. **Food:** Bars and lounges frequently feature complimentary dishes of mixed nuts, spicy chips, and other salt-laden goodies designed to increase your thirst and the size of the bar tab you run up. All of these foods need to be checked for kosher certification, as do many of the beverages you may be drinking.

2. **Beverages:** *Beer*: If you look at the ingredients on a bottle of beer, you will find hops, rice, barley, and that's about it. What you won't find are the other fifty-nine ingredients that breweries are allowed to add to their products without including them on the list of ingredients. Thankfully, there is no cause for panic here and if you like beer, you are in good shape. All major domestic beers and ales, as well as Canadian, Norwegian, English, and German beers, are kosher. The same is true for the increasingly popular microbrews. So enjoy, but remember, never drink and drive. (For a technical explanation of why beer requires no kosher supervision visit Star-K on-line at www.star-k.org.) The beers that *do*

need kosher supervision are any flavored or spiced beers and English stouts.

Liquor: The process of making hard liquors involves three steps: fermentation, distillation, and aging. For the most part, nothing that takes place during any of these three processes can compromise the kashrut of the beverage. The one potential problem area is the aging process. In some instances, casks that have been used to store nonkosher wines are used later to age certain whiskies. If a brand advertises that its liquor is aged in casks, it's advisable to check further before drinking. Another potential problem with some whiskies is actually a taxation issue with kosher implications. In the United States and Canada, wine products are taxed at a lower rate than hard liquor. As a result, liquor manufacturers add small amounts of wine to some of their products in order to avoid the higher tax rates, and these wines may be nonkosher. The bottom line, however, is that more than enough hard liquors are available to the kosher consumer.

The general rules regarding liquor are as follows: All domestic and Canadian whiskies and bourbons are kosher. Scotch and Irish whiskies are also kosher unless the label specifically says that they were aged in sherry or port casks. All gins are kosher. American vodkas are kosher, but imported vodkas require kosher certification. Silver tequilas are kosher, while dark and aged tequilas need certification.

Wine, Liqueur, and Beyond: All wines, champagnes, liqueurs, cordials, brandies, cognacs, rums, and other flavored alcoholic beverages require kosher certification.

3. **Bar Items:** Anything used by a bartender to prepare a mixed drink, including olives, juices, canned mixes, and maraschino cherries, require kosher supervision. And

what if you can't find out if these items are kosher or not? Then just order your drink on the rocks.

Coffee Shop

1. **Food:** This is straightforward: If the coffee shop isn't a certified kosher establishment, then any prepared foods or baked goods brought in from an outside food provider aren't kosher. Packaged foods that have a certified kosher symbol are kosher, and the rest aren't. As a general rule, in coffee shops such as Starbucks, Seattle's Best, and Caribou, you can't eat much other than an occasional granola bar. If you are a Dunkin' Donuts or Krispy Kreme fan, you will be glad to know that a handful of establishments located near large Jewish communities are under kosher supervision. To find out if there is a kosher Dunkin' Donuts or Krispy Kreme in your area, call the local kosher supervisory organization that oversees restaurants and caterers.

2. **Beverages:** So what about your favorite "Cuppa' Joe"? Fresh-brewed coffees are kosher. Where you need to be careful is in adding other ingredients to your coffee. Essentially, it's like this: milk is kosher, though cream and nondairy creamers need kosher certification. Since milk is kosher, your beloved latte and cappuccino are also kosher. Flavorings, however, are a problem. Both flavored coffee beans and liquid coffee flavors need to be certified kosher. Whipped cream, chocolate powders and syrups, and caramel and other toppings also need to be certified kosher. Sugar does not require special kosher certification. And by the way, make sure to get your coffee in a paper cup and not in a mug. For stirring, use a wooden or plastic stirrer and not a metal spoon.

   If you are a tea drinker, you are also in pretty good shape. If you are a fan of the venerable Earl Grey teas, no problem; they are kosher. Green and herbal teas are also kosher as long as they are unflavored. Flavored teas, like flavored coffees, need to be certified kosher. Milk and sugar are kosher, though honey may not be.

HOSTING A KOSHER SUPER BOWL PARTY (GUESTS AT YOUR HOME)

For the snack food industry, sales for Super Bowl Sunday are second only to those for New Year's Eve. If you religiously host a great Super Bowl party and are nervous about what is going to happen now that you are kosher, rest assured; the party—and the game—will go on. Kosher salsa, tortilla chips, beer, honey mustard pretzels, and just about anything else you might want to serve are all readily available. In general, you will find that keeping kosher is little if any hindrance to hosting a good party of any kind. Where matters do get tricky is when well-meaning friends want to pitch in and bring some food of their own to the party. In this situation, you have three options:

1. **Educate them:** Explain to your friends that now that you keep kosher you can serve only certain brands of foods in your home and that these brands are identified by certain symbols printed on the packaging. You can either explain what a few of those symbols look like or invite your friends over and show them some examples. Once you have done this, you can ask your friends to bring items that you know are readily available with a *hechsher*.

2. **Offer your kitchen:** If a friend wants to prepare a dish at home and bring it to your party, explain why that just won't work. "You mean even if I make my meat sauce with kosher ground beef, I still can't bring it to your place?" "I'm afraid not. Kosher cooking goes beyond just the ingredients and even includes food being cooked in kosher pots and pans. It is so nice of you to offer though.

Why don't you come by my place Sunday morning and do the cooking here?"

3. **Suggest kosher wings to go:** Today, many kosher restaurants feature great Super Bowl carry-out menus featuring wings, sauces, and everything in between. You can certainly ask your friends to order a tray or two from such a restaurant. All of these options, with creative variations, can be applied to Thanksgiving dinner, a Fourth of July barbecue, or just about any other event.

Myths&
Facts

Myth: Kosher pastrami is the most delicious pastrami on the planet.

Fact: It depends whom you ask, but if it's not the pastrami, then it's definitely the corned beef. As Uncle Jack used to say about a good pastrami on rye, it's "to die for." (And he probably did.)

NON-JEWISH FRIENDS AND NEIGHBORS

You will find that the vast majority of your non-Jewish friends will be very understanding and respectful of your choice to be more committed to your religion. That people of diverse backgrounds genuinely admire and respect one another's religious commitments and will go out of their way to honor those commitments is truly one of the great blessings of living in a pluralistic society.

In the case of close friends, you will have to address their concern that your new commitment to kosher will put a crimp in your friendship, and in a certain way, it will. Nonetheless, if you employ creative versions of the strategies listed above, along with a pinch of goodwill and common sense, you will find that in the long run, your commitment to kosher will only enhance your relationships as it enhances your life.

CHILDREN'S ISSUES

It's one thing for an adult to start keeping kosher and to deal with all the issues involved; it's quite another for a child. Not only do children face the challenge of being different from their peers, but some children aren't exactly thrilled by their parents' decision to change the rules on them in midstream.

Please keep in mind that this is not a book on effective parenting; therefore, only general principles and suggestions are offered here. Specific applications will vary greatly from family to family, and where teenagers are involved, your guess is as good as mine.

They Don't Want to Go Along

The decision to keep kosher can be a wonderfully positive and transformative event in the life of a Jewish family. Younger children may whine and complain about the change, especially when they find out that they can no longer have their favorite Pop-Tarts, but for the most part they will be flexible and go along with whatever guidelines their parents establish. As a rule, if children see that their parents are sincere and enthusiastic about keeping kosher and about Judaism, then they too will view it in a positive light. Jewish life is meant to be a joy and an inspiration, and it is the job of parents to lead the way in the Jewish home.

Teenagers, however, are wild cards. For parents to succeed in having their teens also "become kosher," it is critical that they include their children in the entire process and not just in the final moment-of-truth decision. Parents who speak with their children about why they are thinking of keeping kosher, and about why Judaism is becoming more important to them, have a good chance of having their children either join them or at least be supportive.

In some instances, no matter how communicative and inclusive parents are, teenage children will do what teenagers do: resent and rebel. In such cases, parents can take three approaches:

- **Force it down their throats:** As parents, you could make the following statement: "We're the parents, you are the children, and as long as you are living in this house you will follow our rules. Our rules are no smoking, no drinking, and no drugs—not in our home and not when you are out with your friends—and those rules now also include no nonkosher food, period. End of discussion. We have nothing further to talk about." If that is the approach you take, then you will probably have as much success with kosher as you will with smoking, drinking, and drugs.

- **Meet them halfway:** It's not unreasonable for a teenager whose parents decide to keep kosher to feel like she is being asked to commit to an awfully big lifestyle change without having the benefit of making the decision for herself. And that is precisely what teens want to do— make decisions for themselves.

  You may very well need to give your teenagers the space to work out this kosher issue on their own terms. This will entail allowing your teens to move at their own pace in deciding if, and to what extent, they want to keep kosher. Practically speaking, you may want to tell your teens that while kashrut will now be observed at home, they are free to do what they want to do when they are at school, at someone else's home, or out with their friends. The message is one of mutual respect: you respect the fact that just as you had to go through a process of learning and thinking before you became fully committed to keeping kosher, they need to go through a similar process in a manner and at a pace that is appropriate for them. At the same time, you expect them to respect the fact that their home is now kosher, and they need to be mindful of all that involves so that they don't "*treif* up the kitchen."

• **Meet them more than halfway:** You may need to lovingly tolerate your children who continue to eat nonkosher food even in your home. Obviously, this is a lot trickier, and you run the risk of kosher and nonkosher foods or cookware becoming mixed together. If you choose this approach, then it is vital that you establish certain parameters regarding where nonkosher foods will be kept, what dishes will be used, where utensils will be stored, and the like.

It's Just Too Hard at a Friend's House

What if you have a child who is perfectly happy to keep kosher but is just too uncomfortable to tell his friends that this is what he does now? This is an area where careful judgment is required. On the one hand, you want to encourage your child to be proud and confident enough about his Judaism that he can maintain his commitment, even when it is uncomfortable. On the other hand, you don't want to push him so far beyond his comfort range that you risk triggering a backlash. The right approach is somewhere in between and will be slightly different in every situation. My advice: say a prayer, hug your kid, and do your best.

An Invitation to a Nonkosher Birthday Party

Let's say your family now keeps kosher and your child has been invited to a birthday party at a nonkosher home. What do you do? The best-case scenario is that you call the other parents, explain your predicament, and tell them that all they need to do is order their birthday cake from a kosher bakery (or from most

Baskin-Robbins stores), and everything else will probably be okay. Most likely, they will be using paper plates and plastic utensils. All the soda they are planning to serve is kosher, and so are most ice creams. You can even offer to pitch in and buy kosher ice cream for the party. Ninety-nine times out of a hundred, you will encounter no resistance and quite often, respectful understanding.

When Children Keep Kosher and Parents Don't

As a parent, you strive not only to care for your children's physical well-being but also to give them certain values that will guide them through life. To the extent that your children embrace your values, you will feel that you are being a successful parent. If they reject your values, you not only may become fearful for them, but also may take their rejection quite personally. Some of the values you communicate to your children are Jewish. By attitude and by example, you let your children know how significant or insignificant a part of life you consider Judaism to be.

Let's say your child decides that she wants to keep kosher, but you don't. What should you do? Once again, a few approaches are possible:

- **Get defensive and dig in your heels:** You could take your child's decision to keep kosher as a slap in the face, let her know that you consider her decision to be an offensive rejection of you personally, and say something like this: "What makes you think you know better than I do? You suddenly think you are so holy. Well, let me tell you something—this is just a phase, and a dangerous one at that, because being too Jewish is just going to get in the way of what's really important in life. Not only that, but it's going to tear the whole family apart. So knock it off."

  If your relationship with your child is already severely strained, then this is the perfect approach. If it's not, then take a deep breath and think twice before saying the wrong thing.

• **Celebrate your child's decision:** If your child came home one night and told you all his friends were getting high but he decided not to join them, you would be proud of him. You would be thrilled that he had the moral clarity and the strength to exercise good judgment. Perhaps you should view kosher in a similar fashion. A young person who decides to keep kosher is essentially making the following statement: "Judaism is more important to me than I ever realized. I know that keeping kosher will put me in some very awkward situations, both with my family and with my friends, but it's worth it to me. I love being Jewish and I'm committed to doing what my ancestors did for thousands of years: eat only kosher food, even if it was far less than the convenient thing to do." Such a statement takes a lot of guts, particularly for a teenager. This kind of inner conviction is something parents ought to celebrate because regardless of whether or not the parents ever keep kosher, it's probably an indication that they have done a good job raising their child.

• **Be supportive:** If you decide to support your child in this decision, you will then have to decide on the practical issues of how this will work. You have two options. The first option is to go through the entire process of koshering your home. This means that you will be keeping kosher at home. What you do outside your home, of course, is up to you. The second option is to accommodate your child by purchasing new cookware that you will use whenever you make kosher meals. In essence, you will be setting up a kosher kitchen within a nonkosher environment. This isn't simple, but it's not as hard as it sounds either. The easiest way to do this is by consulting with a rabbi and implementing his instructions. Keep in mind three factors: (1) self-cleaning ovens, microwave ovens, and stovetop burners can be used for both kosher and nonkosher foods if you know what you are doing; (2) as long as you are using kosher ingredients and kosher cookware, it's no more difficult to make a kosher pot of spaghetti than it is a nonkosher one; and (3) paper plates are one of God's great gifts to the Jewish people, so use them.

Myths & Facts

Myth: The reason kosher symbols are put on plain bottled water is because this is one of the ways the rabbis get more money out of these companies.

Fact: Food companies want kosher supervision on products, whether the product needs it or not, because it's good for business.

Consumers spend approximately $7 billion a year on kosher food, and only 45 percent of the market are Jewish buyers who purchase kosher food for religious reasons. Market researchers have found that 25 percent of consumers believe that kosher certification means the food is of a higher quality. In today's marketplace, where consumers are very conscious about the ingredients and quality of food, kosher certification represents a strong marketing tool.

Muslim consumers represent 20 percent of the kosher market. This is because many of the Islamic dietary laws, known as "Halal," are somewhat similar to kosher laws. Muslims know that if it's kosher for the Jews, then it's "kosher" for them too. Seventh-Day Adventists and other Christian groups whose members don't eat meat know they can rely on pareve kosher foods to be meat free. The same is true in the case of vegetarians. In the case of people with lactose intolerance or severe sensitivities to dairy products, they too know that if it's kosher and pareve, it's safe for them. For all of these reasons, manufacturers want kosher certification on products that—from a Jewish perspective—don't need them.[5]

Chapter 4
More Soul for the Food

In this chapter, we will be exploring a realm that includes kosher and at the same time goes far beyond kosher. Kosher food is about what we eat; this section is about the very activity of eating itself. It's about the deeper meaning of eating, about the essence of our relationship to food, and about how eating can unlock levels of spirituality that we would never expect to be associated with something as simple as biting into a pear, preparing an omelette, or enjoying a glass of wine.

FROM DINING TO A DEEPER LOOK AT EATING

[I] MYSTICAL MUNCHIES

Comedian Jackie Mason has made a career out of making people, mostly Jews, laugh about the differences between Jews and Gentiles. Some of his funniest routines are about Jews' relationship to food. Here are two examples:

When most people return from Europe, they tell tales of all the sites they saw, the shopping, the entertainment . . . Jews, on the other hand, return and say "I had this slice of cake in Austria, let me tell you, I don't know how they make it! It was great!

It is easy to tell the difference between Jews and Gentiles. After the show, all the gentiles are saying "Have a drink? Want a drink? Let's have a drink!" While all the Jews are saying "Have you eaten yet? Let's have coffee and cake!

There is truth to what Mr. Mason is saying: Jews *are* a very food-focused people, and not without a very good and very profound reason.

Myths & Facts

Myth: Kosher means the food was blessed by a rabbi.

Fact: It may be a blessing to eat kosher, but a rabbi doesn't ever need to bless the food to make it kosher. As long as food is prepared in accordance with Jewish law, it's kosher.

BACK TO THE GARDEN: THE HISTORY OF FOOD

The story of food is as old as the story of mankind itself. In fact, according to Judaism's mystical teachings, man's relationship to food is at the heart of understanding existence at its deepest, most esoteric level. To gain an understanding of this relationship, we will need to go back in time, all the way to the sixth day of Creation and the Garden of Eden. Let's take a look:

And God created the human being in His image, in the image of God He created him, male and female He created them. And God blessed them and said to them, "Be fruitful and multiply; fill the earth and master it . . . " And God said, "I have given you all seeded vegetation that is on the face of the earth, and tree that produces seed-bearing fruit; it will be yours to eat. And also to every animal on the earth, every bird in the sky, and to every moving creature on the earth in which there is a living soul; green vegetation will be its food."

Gen. 1:27–30

After introducing Himself to Adam and Eve, one of the very first issues God discussed with them was their diet. A short while later, He told them that there was one particular tree whose fruit they were not allowed to eat:

And God took Adam and placed him in the garden of Eden to work it and to preserve it. And God commanded Adam and said, "You are permitted to eat from all the trees in the garden. However, you are not permitted to eat from the tree of the knowledge of good and evil because on the day you eat from it you will die."

Gen. 2:15–16

In a sense, the story of man's relationship with God begins with a primordial command to keep kosher. This wasn't kosher in the full sense that we know it, but it was kosher in the sense that some foods were permitted and some were not. Whether or not you ever read the Torah, you probably know that despite God's prohibition, Adam and Eve went ahead and ate anyway, and the results weren't pretty:

And God said to Adam, "Because you listened to your wife and went ahead and ate from the tree that I told you not to eat from; the ground will be cursed because of you and for the rest of your life you will eat of it only through suffering. Thorns and thistles is what it will sprout for you and you will eat grasses from the field. Only by the sweat of your brow will you eat bread: And this is how it will be until you yourself return to the ground because you were originally made from the ground—you are dust—and to this dust will you return.

Gen. 3:17–19

Man's relationship to food before eating from the tree of knowledge and man's relationship after were as different as night and day. It is clear from the Torah that before the big blunder, the acquisition of breakfast, lunch, and dinner was a relatively effortless matter. Following the blunder, it became a laborious and arduous task just to put a decent meal on the table. Beyond what is apparent from the text, our tradition tells us that Adam and Eve originally lived in the midst of the most fantastic dining experience one can imagine. Their surroundings were absolutely beautiful, and delicious fruits hung from the branches of trees everywhere. If anyone was ever born with a proverbial silver spoon, it was Adam and Eve. And it goes even further than that. According to the Talmud, "The celestial angels roasted meat for Adam and filtered his wine" (Sanhedrin 59b).

Imagine that. The waiters and chefs where Adam and Eve dined were spiritual beings, and the food, of course, was literally out of this world. Something very deep is being alluded to here: the first human beings were people who were so profoundly in touch with their souls that the way they related to their bodies was similar to the way we relate to our pajamas. We need to have pajamas, but we barely give them any thought. To Adam and Eve, their souls and their intense awareness of God were the essence and focus of their lives. They lived and breathed Godliness in everything they did, and the physical world they inhabited reflected this. They were such genuinely spiritual people that they barely even noticed they had physical needs at all.

The food that nourished them mirrored their state of being. Food was part of their physical reality but tenuously so. It grew by itself, it was all fruit and no chaff or waste, and it was so refined that only an angelic chef knew how to prepare it. Today, we look to food to nourish our bodies, titillate our senses, and perhaps provide a sense of comfort and respite. Back in the garden, food was something altogether different. It was soul food that just happened to also nourish the body.

Just one sip will cost you six hours

After eating meat, one must wait six hours before eating dairy. (A few communities have a custom of waiting less time.) This waiting is required even if you had just a tiny bite of meat. The same is true for something like chicken broth that no longer contains any chicken but was originally cooked with chicken. However, a pareve dish, such as vegetable soup, cooked in a meat pot does not necessitate waiting after eating the soup.

The Mess They Made

The moment Adam and Eve ate from the forbidden tree, everything changed. From that point, it was only a matter of time until we would have wars fought over irrigable lands, a restaurant chain selling billions and billions of hamburgers, and low-fat, protein-packed, high-fiber, whole-grain blueberry muffins. As a result of eating what God warned them not to, Adam and Eve became much more like you and me than like the angels who once did their cooking. It was no longer clear that the soul represented life's highest values and goals while the body was there simply to lend a capable helping hand. Where once the distinction between light and dark was plain to see, the world was now plunged into a sea of gray. It was as if the very fabric of creation had been ripped open, leaving behind an ugly, ragged scar.

Thanks to Adam and Eve, the world became a very flawed place and the lives we lead were fundamentally altered. Today, the soul and the body are forever vying for attention. Our souls pull us in one direction, to God and to being kind, compassionate, and giving, while our bodies drag us elsewhere, to mocha lattes topped with whipped cream and a caramel swirl, to a preoccupation with fashion, to self-centeredness, and to mediocrity. Reality has been inverted. Today, the body and its appetites reign supreme while the soul struggles to find moments here and there to express itself. Today, instead of angels in the kitchen, we've got guys with funny pants and hats.

Tikkun: Their Mess, Our Clean-up Job

Eating food was the vehicle through which the world lost its way, and food and eating are central to repairing the damage. The Hebrew term for cosmic, spiritual repair is *tikkun*, and according to the masters of kabbalistic wisdom, it is the process of *tikkun* that underlies the Jewish relationship to food.

Originally, all the food in the world was perfectly suited for the needs of people living at the most sublime and rarefied level of spirituality. Today, our food still has a dimension that is good for the soul, but it also contains a lot of junk. The mystics refer to the aspect that nourishes the soul as *tov*, "good," and the junk they call *rah*, "bad." Food can be a vehicle by which we are elevated spiritually (and that's a good thing), or it can embolden our physicality and dull our deepest yearnings (and that's a bad thing).

We are all faced with the challenge of breathing spirituality into a world encrusted by thick, coarse layers of physicality. This is the challenge of *tikkun*, of repair, and it begins with each and every one of us. Before we can restore spirituality to its proper place in the world, we must first restore it to its proper place in our own lives, and for that to happen, one of the most important skills we need to learn is how to eat.

The Enlightened Stomach

A kabbalistic synonym for *tov* (good) is *ohr*, which means "light." The corresponding term for *rah* (bad) is *choshech*, which means "darkness." (Note: Before going on, keep in mind that kabbalistic terms are not meant to be taken literally. Rather, their purpose is to convey some sense, even if that is just a vague sense, of a dynamic spiritual dimension that is beyond our ability to truly grasp. The "light" of kabbala is something far different from the light of the sun or the light that fills a room with the flip of a switch. And "darkness" has nothing to do with what happens when the switch is turned to off.)

The mystical writings teach that the singular, fundamental "raw material" for creation is *ohr*, light. The "tools" God worked with to create everything were the twenty-two letters of the Hebrew alphabet. Hebrew letters are repositories of the light of creation. If God is the master artist at work, then His palette is awash in light, and every brush is another letter.

When creation was completed and man was placed in the garden, his task was nothing less than to become God's partner in creation. The mission and the opportunity that Adam and Eve were given was to add to the light of creation. By eating from the tree of knowledge, they failed in their mission, and instead of bringing light into the world, they ushered in an era of darkness. The result was a world in need of *tikkun*, repair—a repair that would have to come through light and food.

Rabbi Yehudah taught that the "tree" from which Adam ate was actually wheat; for a child does not know how to say 'father' or 'mother' until it tastes bread.

Early medrashic teaching

Rabbi Chaim ben Attar lived in Morocco during the first half of the eighteenth century before settling in Israel. In Jerusalem, Rabbi Attar wrote a classic commentary on the Torah in which he often provided glimpses into the kabbalistic meaning of the text. The name of his commentary is *Ohr Hachayim*, the *Light of Life*.

The *Ohr Hachayim* notes that the Hebrew word for wheat, *chita*, has the numerical value of twenty-two (*chet* = 8, *tet* = 9, *heh* = 5). It also notes that every Torah scroll is written with the twenty-two light-bearing letters of the Hebrew alphabet.

It seems that the light that was diminished through the eating of wheat is related to the light of the Torah:

All foods, at the deepest, most elemental level, are nourished from the sanctity of the Torah. From the time that Adam damaged the world, a portion of the *rah* [bad] became mixed into all foods. For this reason wheat now has stubble and chaff that are discarded, and for this reason God commanded us not to eat certain foods that can damage our souls.

Yad Ohr Hachayim, Gen.

From the *Ohr Hachayim* we learn that in a realm that most of us are totally unaware of, there is a deep connection between Torah—which is *light*—and food. Consider the following perplexing statement authored by King David:

To fulfill your will, my God, this is what I have desired; and Your Torah is in my innermost organs.

King David, Psalms, 40:9

The most renowned and influential kabbalistic teacher of the last thousand years was Rabbi Isaac Luria, the Ari. He lived in Safed, Israel, in the mid-sixteenth century. The *Ohr Hachayim* attributes the following teaching to the Ari:

> When one is vigilant not to eat forbidden foods, his inner longing for spirituality will grow stronger. This is what King David was alluding to when he said, *"To fulfill your will, my God, this is what I have desired."* David was referring to his desire to be careful with God's dietary laws, and in that way, *"Your Torah is in my innermost organs."*

Veggie bugs

All vegetables are kosher; however, certain vegetables are regularly infested with tiny insects, such as aphids, thrips, and worms, which are not at all kosher. There are various methods for checking and cleaning different vegetables. (Visit the Star-K Web site for a complete description of how to check vegetables.)

King David was telling us something exceptionally profound about food. He was telling us that when eaten properly, the very food that we eat has the ability to infuse our being with Torah, with the twenty-two little lights that are the soul of the Torah. And so the darkness that descended on mankind and on food through eating can be displaced and repaired by the *light* of Torah—through eating.

Tikkun: Let's Get Practical

For a Jew, there are two types of food in the world. One type includes those foods that are so polluted with *rah* that they are totally off-limits. The only way they can be repaired is from a distance. Every time we respond to God's calling, exert our will, and stay away from impermissible foods, then whatever *good* and whatever *light* are locked in these foods are liberated and actualized by our *not* eating them. In this way, we effect a type of remote *tikkun*. The other kind of foods are those that, while they contain both *tov* and *rah*, have the potential to be infused and elevated with even more *tov* and in that way achieve a positive *tikkun*. *Tikkun* can be effected in permissible foods in a number of different ways. The following are some examples:

> • **Eating kosher food:** The very fact that kosher food is prepared and eaten in accordance with the teaching of the Torah itself creates a *tikkun*.

> • *Kavanah*—eating with directed consciousness: Eating with a specific intent to use the nutrition and energy from food to fuel meaningful, moral, and spiritual endeavors has a powerful elevating effect.

> • **Blessings:** (The topic of blessings is dealt with at length on page 104.) The saying of blessings before and after eating is the ideal means through which to elevate food and eating.

> • **The study of Torah:** A strong, ancient, and widely practiced tradition is to study and discuss classic Jewish texts at a meal. Even if this is done for just a few brief moments, it not only infuses our meal with meaning but also transforms our meal into something akin to eating in the holy Temple that once stood in Jerusalem.

There is a wonderful story about one of the Chassidic masters, a disciple, and the blessing for eating an apple. A student came to his *rebbe* and said, "Rebbe, I make a blessing and you make a blessing; I eat an apple and you eat an apple. Is there really any difference between us?" To which the *rebbe* responded, "You make a blessing so you can eat the apple. I eat the apple so I can make a blessing."

[II] KEDUSHA: HOLINESS BEGINS IN THE KITCHEN

We are about to consider the meaning and implications of a word that represents a deeply important dimension of Judaism. The word is *holiness*, and while it is a defining element of Jewish life, for most, its meaning remains a mystery. In the realm of kosher, holiness is central, though here too its meaning is murky, if not completely baffling. I'd like you to think of the next few pages as a kind of exploration, as a search for the meaning of holiness in Judaism.

NOT AS HOLY AS THOU

In the course of our exploration into holiness, one of our most important tools will be the Hebrew language. For this reason, we will need to stop using the word holiness and switch to the Hebrew word *kedusha*. At first you may find this usage of the word *kedusha* to be a bit awkward, but trust me, it's essential. You see, the English word *holiness* has so many associations and is used in so many different contexts that it's impossible for it not to conjure up all sorts of ideas other than what it means in Judaism. So we'll use the word *kedusha* because it is a beautiful Hebrew word laden with uniquely Jewish meaning.

Let's begin our exploration with a survey of the centrality of kedusha to Judaism.

Kadosh—The Defining of a Nation

The defining (and coolest) event in all of Jewish history took place when God gave the Torah to the Jewish nation at Mount

Sinai. It was there that God told millions of Jews what kind of a
nation He wanted them to be:

*And you will have a relationship with Me that is unique and distinct
from all other nations. . . . And you will be a kingdom of priests and a
holy [kadosh] nation.*

Exod. 19:5–6

The word **kadosh**, and the word *kedusha*, have the same root
meaning. There, at the foot of Sinai, the Jewish people were
informed that the unique, overarching quality of *kedusha* would
distinguish them as a people for all time.

Mikdosh—A Condo for God

After giving the Torah to the Jewish people, God told them
to launch the most important construction project in history. The
structure they were instructed to build was called a *mikdosh*.
Sound familiar?

To appreciate the true meaning of this *mikdosh* project, we
need a context. Without a context, relating to the *mikdosh* would
be like watching magnificent new buildings going up at Ground
Zero without having any idea of what took place on 9/11. In the
case of the *mikdosh*, the context is the basic paradigm for God's
relationship to the world He created. In essence, the paradigm is
this: when God finished creating the world, He wasn't quite
done. Incredibly, instead of completing the job Himself, the
finishing touches of creation were left to mankind. Our sages put
it as follows: "God desired that there be a place for Him to dwell
within the world He created." This means that while God had
created a world and then put people in it, what He was now
asking of those people was that they turn around and build a
world that He could also feel comfortable in. To make a long
story short, mankind failed to build a suitable neighborhood for
God, and so He gave the job to a fledgling Jewish construction
firm headed by a man named Moses.

Shortly after giving them the Torah, God told the Jewish people that they were to construct an abode where the Divine Presence would be particularly and intensely manifest in the world. This is what He said:

> And God spoke to Moses, saying, Speak to the children of Israel and from everyone who desires, take a donation for me. The donation you take from them will be: gold, silver, and copper; turquoise, purple and red wool, linen. . . And you will make for me a holy sanctuary [*mikdosh*], and My Presence will rest amongst you.
>
> Exod. 25:9

The word **mikdosh** and the word *kedusha* have the same root meaning. This **mikdosh** was first constructed in the desert and later found its permanent home in the Temple in Jerusalem. It was a crowning achievement for the Jewish people and a place where God's transcendent reality could somehow be manifest in a world fashioned by both God and man.

Kidoshim—Be Like Me

After receiving the Torah from God, Moses had a lot of teaching to do. As a rule, he would teach a lesson first to his brother Aaron and his sons, then to a group of distinguished elders, and finally to the nation as a whole. This is how he did it for hundreds and hundreds of lessons until one day God told Moses to modify the teaching process for one pivotal lesson:

> *God spoke to Moses and said, 'Speak to the entire assembly of the Children of Israel and say to them: You shall be kadosh (holy), because I am kadosh, the Lord your God.*
>
> Lev. 19:1–2

Again, the word **kadosh** and the word *kedusha* have the same root meaning. It seems that the call to *kedusha* is so particularly significant that God wanted it to be taught immediately to the entire nation. The reason for this, as explained by our sages, is that aspiring and striving for *kedusha* is a seminal value intended to permeate virtually all of Jewish life. The collective persona and culture of the Jewish people is *kedusha*. The presence of *kedusha* transforms commandments from just another set of laws into a holistic lifestyle designed to imbue all things Jewish with the luster of *kedusha*.

A Different Brand of Holiness

Moses Maimonides lived in Egypt in the twelfth century and is one of the most important and influential scholars of the last thousand years. In addition to being a highly regarded doctor, authoring numerous books on medicine and serving as the personal physician to the sultan and his family, Maimonides was the first person to write a comprehensive, systematic code of Jewish law. This great work is known as the Mishne Torah. In fourteen volumes, the Mishne Torah thoroughly covers the full gamut of all the laws in the Torah.

One of the volumes in the Mishne Torah is the Book of Kedusha. Curiously, the Book of Kedusha seems to deal with none of the topics that one might expect to find under the topic of *kedusha*. There is no mention of the Temple in Jerusalem, no mention of prayer, and nothing about *Shabbat* or the holidays. Oddly enough, the only three topics included are kosher foods, kosher sexual relations, and the laws of kosher slaughtering. Maimonides seems to tell us something counterintuitive: *kedusha* has more to do with the kitchen and the bedroom than with the synagogue and the study hall. But how can this be? How can something as lofty, as spiritual, and as Godly as *kedusha* be rooted in matters so utterly pedestrian?

The answer lies in the Jewish view of the relationship between the physical dimension of life and the spiritual dimension. Often, when people think of spirituality and physicality, they think in terms of a dichotomy that places the two at opposite ends of a spectrum. In this view, the more one embraces the spiritual, the further one moves from the physical. The reverse is also assumed to be true. Maimonides, however, tells us to think in different terms. We should consider a view of human beings that sees beyond physicality and spirituality as polar opposites to not only a place where the two exist in harmony but where their harmony is essential to *kedusha*.

Holy Bagels

We all have physical needs and urges as well as higher needs and loftier aspirations. Yes, we need to eat and we want to enjoy our food, but we also need to feel that our lives are as filled with meaning as our stomachs are with bagels, cream cheese, and coffee. We want to do good and be good, not just eat good. We want to teach our children that even the pleasure of their favorite meal pales next to the pleasure of providing a meal for someone who has nothing to eat at all. The same is true with marital intimacy. We have a drive and needs, and we want to have an enjoyable intimate life—but not at the expense of demeaning another human being or ourselves. People's drives may lead to all sorts of wishful thinking, but not a single healthy human being would choose night after night of loveless liaisons over a lifetime of intimacy with someone he or she cherished dearly. You see, it's our physicality—our bodies—that dream about endless restaurants and endless romances, while our souls dream of close and loving relationships, of having character and integrity, and of lifting and enriching the lives of others.

The great question about our physicality and our spirituality is, Are we locked in a zero-sum struggle or is there room for cooperation? Clearly, what Maimonides wants us to understand is that from a Jewish perspective, not only are the two not mutually exclusive, but spirituality and holiness are to be found, more than anywhere else, in the realm of our most basic physical needs.

The following is not a line from a routine by comedian Jackie Mason: "In Judaism, food and holiness go hand in hand." And I don't mean to make Grandma blush, but marital intimacy and *kedusha* also go hand in hand.

PLANTING AND BUILDING

The Creation Paradigm

Life is about growing, progressing, and climbing higher and higher and higher. It's the antithesis of stagnation and inertia. The means by which we grow, progress, and climb are a reflection of one of Judaism's deepest organizing principles, a principle that touches on the essence of creation itself.

Our understanding of creation is not that in the brilliant flash of one supremely creative moment God brought everything into existence but that in that moment He created the *potential* for all existence. "In the beginning" there was ultimate potential, and from within that potential everything else was formed and revealed. This is the law of spiritual physics: first potential and then unfolding actualization. This principle is not only at the core of creation but also forms the human core. The life of every person reflects this principle. God brings each person into the world the same way He brought the world into being: with unimaginable potential. We come into this world with soaring, near-Divine potential—with almost limitless, albeit hidden, potential. We embark on life as adorable, innocent, delicious bundles of potential, yet, at the same time, we are selfish, self-centered, and hedonistic. The challenge of life is to grow and progress and to actualize our dormant goodness and latent *kedusha*.

Planting and Building

God "planted" within the world great potential, and then He "built" something out of it. God plants and builds, and so do we. We plant and build institutions, projects, and businesses. We plant and build friendships, students, and children. Most of all, we plant and build ourselves.

To plant and build oneself is to create, raise, and nurture a person who looks beyond one's self for the values that order life and who pursues goodness, meaning, and kedusha in endeavors that go beyond the narrow confines of self-gratification. Let me explain.

Myths & Facts

Myth: Deer and buffalo are not kosher because they are wild animals.

Fact: Bambi wasn't wild.

Both deer and buffalo are kosher if they are slaughtered properly. In the age of cholesterol consciousness, the market for kosher bison has grown significantly because it has less cholesterol than beef.

Planting is a subtle, slow, delicate process. Seeds are placed in the soil, they are watered by rains, nourished by the soil and the sun's rays, and with time a plant grows and blossoms. Planting is about values and perspectives that are the seeds of spiritual (*kedusha*-filled) living. The values and perspectives that we surround ourselves with and that inform our choices slowly and steadily seep into the deepest recesses of our being. When we plant new values and perspectives, they eventually blossom into new behaviors.

Building is about the careful placement of behavioral bricks into the structure of life. We build by inserting new bricks—new behavioral routines—into our daily lives. We build by making it a habit to give to charity or to volunteer. We build by going out of our way to show respect to our parents and to the elderly.

Conversely, we also build by removing faulty, worn bricks. We build by confronting a harmful habit and overcoming it. We build when we say no to frivolous indulgences that waste our time, money, and lives. Whenever we add or strengthen a good habit or break a harmful one, we are building. Building is more obvious and more immediate than planting.

Planting *cultivates* human spirituality through cognitive and attitudinal change, while building *constructs* spiritual living through behavioral change.

Ultimately, neither planting nor building alone will produce the results we desire. If we are to bring forth the spiritual greatness that is possible for each of us, then we need to apply both approaches.

Planting and Building Our Way to Kedusha

I don't know about you, but everyone I know struggles with food. Honestly, do you know anyone who finds it easy not to eat half a bag of potato chips once he or she gets started? Do you know anyone who doesn't walk away from the Thanksgiving table without eating too much—usually way too much? Do you know anyone who isn't severely tested by the thought of just one piece of homemade cheesecake?

Today we deal with our struggles with food by dieting, but it wasn't always that way.

In the mid-eighteenth century, Rabbi Moshe Chaim Luzatto, one of the most influential Jewish scholars, mystics, and writers of the last two hundred and fifty years, wrote a treatise on spiritual growth that became a classic. The title of his work is "The Path of the Just" (Mesilat Yesharim), and it is a step-by-step guide to achieving the highest levels of spirituality. In the closing chapters of the book, Rabbi Luzatto addresses our relationship to physical pleasures in general and to food in particular and lays out a three-tiered approach to physicality and *kedusha*.

The following is a very brief summary of this three-tiered approach to *kedusha*. I have divided each level into two parts:

"planting" and "building." Planting is about how we perceive and understand physicality and *kedusha*, and building is about how we implement and actualize *kedusha*. Here goes:

Level I—Separation
• Planting: We all have a natural inclination to experience physical sensations for no other reason than the sheer enjoyment and pleasure we derive from them. Two qualities shared by all physical pleasures create potential problems and pitfalls. 1) The actual pleasure is short-lived. For example, once you have swallowed the cookie, the pleasure is gone. To have more of the same pleasure, you will need to eat another cookie. 2) Too much is bad for you. In the extreme, eating too much can make you sick, lead to obesity, and develop into an addiction. Short of that, food can leave you feeling dull, lethargic, and weighed down instead of energized.

There is nothing wrong with enjoying what you eat, as long as you don't become so enthralled with entertaining your taste buds that what drives you to eat is the frenetic search for titillation instead of the search for nutrition and the energy needed to fuel healthy living.

• Building: To create a healthy relationship with food, you should eat only when you are hungry and eat a bit less than necessary to satisfy your hunger. Eat because you need to, not for the thrill of it.

Level II—Purity
• Planting: While the discipline of separation enables you to master desires rather than being mastered by them, separation is still not liberation. You may be in charge of *when* you eat yet still be overly enthralled with the luscious sensations that are yours once you "dig in." This is where purity comes in. Purity says that the motivation to eat the food in front of me is rooted in my desire to be healthy, energized, strong, and of clear mind and not in

my desire for a Thai, Mexican, or Creole experience. And beyond that, the health and strength benefits I desire are themselves rooted in a higher motivation—the desire to live as meaningful a life as possible—a life of giving, caring, and relating to God.

• Building: With purity, the action is found in thoughtful reflection. One needs to reflect on the values and ideals that are at the core of one's life. One needs to reflect on and feel a sense of mission in life that is so palpable that the pleasure of food—even great food—pales when compared to the pleasure of having the strength to pursue the deeper, richer pleasures of life.

Level III—*Kedusha*

• Planting: Rabbi Luzatto sees *kedusha* as living in partnership with God. The fruit of this partnership is the manifestation of God's presence—God's reality—in and through the physical world. When I look at all of life as a grand opportunity to connect with God, then food as well as all other physical pleasures become vehicles for bringing God into the world. This is where physicality ceases to be any kind of impediment to spirituality and is elevated to the level of harmonious association with spirituality. This is *kedusha*.

• Building: Whatever we do, we do with God in mind. Our mission is to create the kind of "space" in the world that is welcoming to God's presence. The preparation of such a space is *our* contribution to the partnership of *kedusha*, and God's filling of that space is His part. When this occurs, then the physical world—we, our meals, our intimate lives, and everything else—is transformed from the physical and the mundane to the spiritual and the *kodesh* (holy).

MAKE ROOM FOR GOD

We can now understand why Maimonides deals exclusively with food and intimate relations in the Book of Kedusha and why *kedusha* is the central, defining element of Jewish life.

Food can be a person's most bitter enemy. A person who can't control his or her relationship to food is a person who lives to eat instead of one who eats to live. A person whose highest aspirations are physical aspirations is only half a person, if that. Yet the same can be said about spirituality. A person whose reach for spirituality takes a path that denies and denigrates physicality is also only half a person. A whole person is someone who neither degrades the physical in the name of the spiritual nor sullies the spiritual in the hot pursuit of the physical. A whole person, a person of *kedusha*, is one who devotes every dimension of life to the highest achievement possible: to making room in his life, and in this world, for God.

> God's deep "desire" is that His Presence [the Shechina], have a place in the physical world. This can be achieved by relating to God specifically through the physicality of our world, for this is the purpose of the creation of the world—to make out of it a place where God could dwell.
>
> Chassidic master, Rabbi Shalom Noah Berzovski

When God told the Jewish people to build a *mikdosh*, he was saying that while the heavens have plenty of nice suburbs, He really wants to live in our neighborhood. When God defined the Jewish nation as a "kingdom of priests and a holy (*kadosh*) nation," he meant that it would be our mission to transform the world we live in into a world that He too could "live" in. And when God said to each and every Jew, "You shall be *kadosh*," He was telling us that just as the physical world can be elevated, so can we.

HOLY KOSHER

The Torah introduces the laws of kosher food in a lengthy section of the book of Leviticus. The Torah concludes its discussion about what is and isn't kosher by saying, "For I am the Lord your God, you should live a life of *kedusha* and be *kodesh*, for I am *kodesh*." Each subsequent time that the Torah addresses kosher foods, it does so in the context of *kedusha*. The same is true with the laws of intimate relations in the Torah: their context is *kedusha*.

When God linked kosher and intimacy to kedusha, He was telling us that to scale the heights of *kedusha*, we need to make sure that we take the bedroom and the kitchen with us.

[III] LIFE IS A BLESSING, AND SO ARE COOKIES

In Judaism, nine wonderful blessings can be recited both before and after one eats food. One short blessing is said before one begins to eat, and another is said when one is finished. These blessings, while not technically part of what makes food kosher, nonetheless play a prominent role in how we experience and relate to eating. For this reason, we will discuss blessings in general and, more specifically, those blessings that relate to food.

If you happened to be in synagogue for Rosh Hashanah this year, then you may recall that just before the shofar was sounded, the person who was to do the blowing uttered a few lines in Hebrew. These were *b'rachot*, or special blessings, that precede the sounding of the shofar. If you missed Rosh Hashanah, then perhaps you recall the recital of blessings before the lighting of a Chanukah menorah or a blessing or two at a Passover Seder.

B'rachot, blessings, have a special place in the spiritual life of a Jew. In addition to the blessings said during the various holidays, there are a number of beautiful, lesser-known blessings, including those said before smelling a rosebush, after going to the bathroom, when one hears a loud clap of thunder, and at a marriage ceremony. Of all the blessings that are a part of Jewish life, the most ubiquitous are those said before we eat. I'm not just talking about the generic "rub-a-dub-dub, thanks for the grub, yea, God." I'm talking about very specific, very beautiful, and very inspiring blessings. You see, there is a special blessing that one says before eating a piece of fruit; another for vegetables; one for cookies, pretzels, and other baked goods; another for beverages; and so on. The concept of verbally reciting blessings is meant to make an indelible impact on our consciousness.

In Hebrew, the word for blessing, *bracha*, is closely related to the word *breicha*, which means "a natural spring of water." A free-flowing spring of fresh, life-giving water is the Jewish image of a blessing. In many ways it is also the Jewish image of life. The purpose of blessings is to call our attention to spiritually dramatic moments and experiences that often get overlooked.

When one sees a flash of lightning illuminate the sky, the blessing to be recited is, *"Blessed are You God, our Lord, Sovereign of the universe, Who constantly renews creation."* Blessings are tools designed to enable us to truly see what often goes unnoticed— the wonders that are all around us. They sensitize us to the reality that much of what we naturally come to take for granted is actually a profound blessing. They transform seemingly mundane acts into stirring moments of spiritual awareness.

THE SIX MOST COMMON BLESSINGS SAID BEFORE EATING

Following is the text of the six most common blessings said before eating. Each blessing appears in English, Hebrew, and Hebrew transliteration. These blessings are said before one takes the first bite or sip, and each is recited only once for each item or group of items. For example, if you were about to snack on a bowl of cashews, you would say one blessing before eating the first cashew and that would suffice for all the rest. Similarly, if you were having an assortment of nuts or an assortment of fruits, one blessing would apply to everything you eat. Following each blessing in this section is a list of the most common foods associated with that blessing.

It is important to point out that these six blessings represent only a portion of the entire world of food-related blessings. In addition to the blessings said before one eats, three blessings can be said after one eats. A comprehensive study of all the blessings is beyond the scope of this book. The goal of this section is simply to serve as a brief introduction to the food blessings.

IT'S THE LAW!

Now that's a sharp blade

The knife used for *shechita* (ritual slaughtering) must be so sharp that simply sliding the blade on an animal's throat without applying any significant downward pressure makes a clean cut. When a kosher animal is being slaughtered, a clean cut must be made through the trachea and the esophagus. The blade must be checked after every cut to ensure that it is sufficiently sharp so that it won't tear these organs.

The practice of saying blessings before one eats is an exceptionally beautiful aspect of Jewish life. However, if you are not accustomed to saying these blessings, it can be a bit daunting to think about reciting a blessing each and every time you have something to eat. It can also be a bit socially awkward for you to look as if you have suddenly taken to talking to your food. I want to remind you that Judaism is not all-or-nothing and that many people begin by saying blessings only occasionally or saying just one or two blessings a day. If you are in the process of beginning to keep kosher, that is certainly a major commitment, and your food is kosher with or without your saying a blessing. When the time is right and you begin experimenting with blessings, I only hope this section will have served as a meaningful introduction.

THE SIX BLESSINGS

Ha'etz—This blessing is said before eating fruit:

Blessed are You, God, our Lord, Sovereign of the universe, Who creates the fruit of the tree.

בָּרוּךְ אַתָּה יהוה אֱלֹהֵינוּ מֶלֶךְ הָעוֹלָם בּוֹרֵא פְּרִי הָעֵץ

Baruch atah Adonai, Elohaynu melech ha-olam, boray p'ri ha-aytz.

It is said prior to eating oranges, pears, nectarines, kiwis, figs, avocados, apples, and all other fruits, as well as almonds, cashews, and all other nuts except peanuts.

Ha'adamah—This blessing is said before eating vegetables:

Blessed are You, God, our Lord, Sovereign of the universe, Who creates the fruit of the earth.

בָּרוּךְ אַתָּה יהוה אֱלֹהֵינוּ מֶלֶךְ הָעוֹלָם בּוֹרֵא פְּרִי הָאֲדָמָה

Baruch atah Adonai, Elohaynu melech ha-olam, boray p'ri ha-adamah.

It is said prior to eating cucumbers, watermelons, tomatoes, snow peas, potatoes, french fries, cabbages, strawberries, carrots, and peppers; Caeser, Greek, and other salads; peanuts and sunflower seeds; and all other vegetables.

Hamotzi—This blessing is said before eating bread:

Blessed are You, God, our Lord, Sovereign of the universe, Who brings forth bread from the earth.

בָּרוּךְ אַתָּה יהוה אֱלֹהֵינוּ מֶלֶךְ הָעוֹלָם הַמּוֹצִיא לֶחֶם מִן הָאָרֶץ

*Baruch atah Adonai, Elohaynu melech ha-olam,
ha-motzi lechem min ha-aretz.*

It is said prior to eating french, spelt, whole wheat, and all other breads; bagels, pita, and all sandwiches.

Mezonot—This blessing is said before eating grain products:

Blessed are You, God, our Lord, Sovereign of the universe, Who creates a variety of nourishing foods.

בָּרוּךְ אַתָּה יהוה אֱלֹהֵינוּ מֶלֶךְ הָעוֹלָם בּוֹרֵא מִינֵי מְזוֹנוֹת

*Baruch atah Adonai, Elohaynu melech ha-olam,
boray minay m'zonot.*

It is said prior to eating poundcake, cheesecake, and all other cakes; apple, cherry, and all other pies; cookies, rugeluch, donuts, croissants, and just about anything else you can get at a bakery; pasta dishes; pretzels; all oat or wheat breakfast cereals, cereal bars, and granola bars; and rice.

Ha'gafen—This blessing is said before drinking wine or grape juice:

Blessed are You God, our Lord, Sovereign of the universe, Who creates the fruit of the grapevine.

בָּרוּךְ אַתָּה יהוה אֱלֹהֵינוּ מֶלֶךְ הָעוֹלָם בּוֹרֵא פְּרִי הַגָּפֶן

*Baruch atah Adonai, Elohaynu melech ha-olam,
boray p'ri ha-gafen.*

It is said prior to drinking Chardonnay, Merlot, Champagne, and all other wines, as well as grape juice.

Shehakol—This generic blessing is said before partaking of other food or drink:

Blessed are You, God, our Lord, Sovereign of the universe, through Whose word everything came to be.

בָּרוּךְ אַתָּה יהוה אֱלֹהֵינוּ מֶלֶךְ הָעוֹלָם שֶׁהַכֹּל נִהְיֶה בִּדְבָרוֹ

*Baruch atah Adonai, Elohaynu melech ha-olam,
she-hakol nih'yeh b'dvoro.*

It is said prior to eating or drinking anything not included in the more specific blessings above, including all meats, poultry, and fish; Swiss, gouda, and all other cheeses; yogurts and other dairy products; tofu; most candies (except for wafer-based candy bars, whose blessing is Mezonot); ice creams; and juices, water, soda, beer, coffee, and other beverages.

REFLECTIONS
Following are five Jewish perspectives on life and spirituality as revealed through the blessings said for food.

I. The Blessing of Consciousness

Imagine what it would be like if a few times a day, for just a minute or two, you reviewed a list of the most important matters in your life: family, integrity, God, helping a needy friend, the end of the curse of the Billy Goat in Chicago, honesty, Israel. I suspect that with time, slowly but surely, your life would be transformed—perhaps only subtly but beautifully nonetheless. For many of us, our daily preoccupations tend to be with items that, while important and pressing, are not necessarily indicative of our core values and highest priorities in life. This is where blessings come to the rescue. Blessings are like a strong, caring hand that gently reaches out and taps us on the shoulder in the midst of the most common, mundane activity one can think of—eating. Eating food is how we fuel our bodies so that we can carry on with daily living. Blessings for food are how we fuel our consciousness so that we are aware of what it is we are living for.

Let's explore some corners of Jewish consciousness as revealed through the blessings for food.

II. Birkat Hamazon: The Root of All Blessings

You now know that there are six blessings to be said before one eats and a number of others to be said after one eats. I want to take a moment to reflect on the single most important food-related blessing. It's called Birkat Hamazon, the "Blessing for Sustenance," and it is recited after every meal that includes bread.

Birkat Hamazon is particularly significant because it is the only blessing that the Torah itself mandates. As such, Birkat Hamazon serves as the model blessing for all other blessings. All other blessings were instituted by the sages of the Talmud as additional means of achieving what Birkat Hamazon does: it focuses our consciousness on God when we are engaged in eating.

Birkat Hamazon is by far the longest food blessing, and it is actually made up of four subblessings. We will take a look first at the source and context of Birkat Hamazon in the Torah and then at each of the four component blessings. Birkat Hamazon is found in the midst of an address delivered by Moses to the Jewish people at the end of his life, just before they entered the promised land of Israel. (The bold phrase is the source verse for Birkat Hamazon.)

> The entirety of the commandment that I have commanded you today you shall be careful to perform, so that you will live and increase, and enter and possess the land that God promised to your forefathers. And you should remember the entire way that God led you for these forty years in the wilderness . . . and He fed you the special manna—something neither you or your ancestors ever experienced—in order to teach you that not by bread alone does man live, rather by all that emanates from God does man live. . . . **You will eat and be satisfied, and bless the Lord your God for the good land he gave you.** Be careful not to forget God . . . lest you eat and be satisfied and build good homes and settle down. And with a proud heart you will forget the Lord your God who took you out of the land of Egypt. . . . And you will say in your heart, "It is through my own strength and ability that I achieved all this." You should rather remember your God: He is the one who has given you the ability in order to implement the covenant that He swore to your forefathers. . . .
>
> Deut. 8:1–18

From the text of the Torah, the most essential idea contained in Birkat Hamazon—"you will eat and be satisfied, and bless"— is that we need to acknowledge that food is a blessing, that God is the source of that blessing, and that all of our blessings ultimately emanate from God. Now, a brief look at the four parts of Birkat Hamazon.

1. *Hazan:* the blessing for sustenance. In this blessing we recognize that it is God who maintains and sustains everything in creation. We, and all of God's creation, are

nourished by Him alone. Our existence, our lives, our every breath, and our every meal are all part of a relationship with the grand, transcendent source of all existence. And that is truly a blessing to be remembered.

Soul Food

Rabbi Abraham Isaac Kook was chief rabbi in prestate Israel. He taught the following:

"In the land of Israel, the physicality in food is relatively superficial, while its essence is holy. Outside of Israel, the physicality in food is more dominant and therefore one has to be extra careful not only when it comes to eating kosher but also in how one eats.

To the extent that one's inner life is connected to the land of Israel, and to the degree that one longs to be in the Land, he is able to transform the quality of foods outside of Israel to being more like the foods of Israel themselves. And even in Israel itself, when one longs for the time when Jerusalem will be fully restored, this too infuses one's food with a heightened degree of spirituality. It is for this reason that prior to Birkat Hamazon we recite either Al N'harot Bavel (By the Waters of Babylon) or Shir Ha'maalot (the Song of Ascents), both of which are focused on Jerusalem and the land of Israel."

Orot Hakodesh, vol. 3

2. *Ha'aretz:* the blessing for the land of Israel. With this blessing our attention is called to the profound relationship between the unique historic destiny of the Jewish people and the land of Israel. For the Jewish people to feel and experience and realize the deepest, fullest richness of God's blessings we must do so in the "good land."

3. *Yerusholayim:* the blessing for Jerusalem. The Jews are a people of boundless vision and endless hope. Jerusalem is the essence and embodiment of that vision, that dream. For millennia, though Jerusalem lay in ruins and Jews were scattered across the world, the longing to return never moved from the center of Jewish consciousness. Synagogues around the world are all built facing Jerusalem, the focus of our hearts and souls. At the Passover Seder, at the conclusion of the Neila service on Yom Kippur, and when the glass is broken under the chuppah at a wedding, the sentiment is always the same: next year in Jerusalem. And so too with Birkat Hamazon: wherever we are and whenever we thank God for all our blessings, we can't help but train our thoughts on Jerusalem.

4. *Hatov V'hameitiv:* the blessing for past and future good. This blessing was written during a dark and tragic period at the end of the Second Temple Era. Its intended message was that Jews must be aware of God's presence, even in the midst of destruction. In this blessing we not only reflect on the blessing we have just experienced and enjoyed, but we also think about how much God has blessed us in the past, and look forward to His future blessings.

III. Kavanah: Blessings as Meditations

The last twenty years has seen an explosion in the Western world's appreciation of what has come to be known as the mind-body relationship. Thanks to the breakthrough work of people such as Harvard cardiologist Herbert Benson, University of Arizona Medical School professor Andrew Weil, and University of California clinical professor of medicine Dean Ornish (all nice Jewish doctors), meditation has come to be understood as a discipline with profound emotional, spiritual, and even physical implications:

> Meditation is the practice and process of paying attention and focusing your awareness. When you meditate, a number of desirable things begin to happen—slowly, at first, and deepening over time. . . . Anything that you enjoy—food, music, art, massage, and so on—is greatly enhanced by meditation. . . . Finally, you may directly experience and become more aware of the transcendent interconnectedness that already exists. You may have a direct experience of God . . .
>
> Dr. Dean Ornish, M.D., Clinical Professor of Medicine at the University of California, San Francisco, School of Medicine and the bestselling author of *Love and Survival: The Scientific Basis for the Healing Power of Intimacy.*

Myths & Facts

Myth: Kosher and kosher style are the same thing.

Fact: You know those knockoff Gucci purses that sell for sixty dollars instead of three hundred? Well, that's the equivalent of kosher style versus kosher. A kosher style hot dog may look, smell, and taste like a kosher hot dog, but it's definitely not kosher.

Insights that have ushered in a new era of awareness in contemporary society have been intrinsic to Judaism for thousands of years. The observance of eating kosher food and the discipline of approaching food by way of a blessing are built on the awareness of a deep mind-body-soul connection:

> The most common word for meditation in Judaic literature is Kavanah. Looking at the origin of the word Kavanah, we immediately see that it comes from the Hebrew root kaven, which means "to aim." Kavanah denotes "aiming" consciousness toward a certain goal. The most apt translation is "directed consciousness." It is taught that when a person eats, he should concentrate totally on the food and the experience of eating it, clearing the mind of all other thoughts. He should have in mind that the taste of the food is also an expression of the Divine in the food . . . eating itself can be a form of meditation as well as a means through which one can draw closer to God. It was for this reason that it was ordained that a blessing be recited before one begins eating. When a blessing is recited before eating, then the act itself becomes a spiritual undertaking. Through the blessing, the act of eating becomes a contemplative exercise. Judaism sees even the most mundane acts as means of gaining God consciousness.
>
> Rabbi Aryeh Kaplan, *Jewish Meditation: A Practical Guide*

Have you ever become so immersed in an experience that it was as if nothing else in the world existed? Perhaps it was a moment of love: watching your child be born or walking your child to the *chuppah*. Perhaps it was reaching up to touch the stones of that timeless wall in Jerusalem or standing alone outside at the break of dawn, transfixed by an emergent illumination and the sounds of birds at daybreak. If you know that feeling, then you have an inkling of the world that blessings can open up to us. Blessings are the means through which we "aim" and fine-tune our awareness so that a slice of bread, a grape, or a glass of water can be transformed into a portal of deep, spiritual consciousness.

Go ahead, try it.

IV. Hamotzi—The Blessing for Bread

Hamotzi, the blessing said before eating bread, is the most well-known of all the food blessings. The text of hamotzi is as follows:

Blessed are you, God, our Lord, Sovereign of the universe Who brings forth bread from the earth.

If you think about it, this blessing doesn't seem to be giving credit where credit is due. Granted, God brings forth wheat from the ground, but when was the last time you saw a farmer harvesting loaves of bread? Bread comes from the oven, not "from the earth." And if you want to be a stickler about this, you might conclude that God doesn't even deserve all the credit for the wheat. After all, it's the farmer who tills the soil, sows the seeds, and then harvests the crop at just the right time. If anything, the production of bread is a joint venture, with God seeming to be the junior partner.

THE PARTNERSHIP OF MAN AND GOD

Consider this: When I floss my teeth and thereby forestall the creeping advances of tooth and gum decay, do I deserve a pat on the back and a round of applause? Do I hold my head high and flash a proud, contented smile? Or do I say, "Thank God I've got the brains and ability to prevent my teeth from becoming mush."

Judaism says to take pleasure—not pride—in the constructive choices you make in life. The Jewish view of the man-God partnership boils down to this: you make the sensible choice to floss your teeth; the rest is a gift. The cognitive aptitude necessary to grasp the hygienist's instructions on how to floss, the ability to consistently judge whether or not you've pulled out the right amount of floss, the dexterity required to gently maneuver the floss between tooth and gum—each of these remarkable talents, along with countless others, is a gift from

God. Our job is to recognize the abundant shower of blessings He has granted us, to be grateful, and to partner with God.

A fresh loaf of bread, like a well-flossed tooth, is a marvelous accomplishment. Each time we say Hamotzi, we are reminded to take pleasure in our accomplishments and to be thankful that we have chosen to use our many gifts in a morally refined, spiritually elevated, and meaningful manner.

IT'S THE LAW!

Fish and meat

Although the Torah does not forbid eating meat and fish together, the Talmud teaches that the two should not be eaten together. This prohibition does not carry with it the same stringencies related to milk and meat. Therefore, a fish dish can be prepared in either a milk pot or a meat pot. One can also eat milk together with fish.

V. Shehakol: Spark of Creation

The blessing of *shehakol* is a generic, catchall blessing that covers any foods missed by the more specific blessings. Also, if one mistakenly replaces any of the other blessings with *shehakol*, that's not a problem because it can apply to anything. The text of *shehakol* is as follows:

> *Blessed are You God, our Lord, Sovereign of the universe,*
> *through Whose word everything came to be.*

As unassuming as it seems to be, *shehakol* actually packs quite a punch.

The implication of "through Whose word everything came to be" is that everything that exists does so because God wants it to exist. God's "wanting" things to exist means that they have a very specific purpose, that this purpose is meaningful to none less than the Creator Himself, and that He cares about and is interested in what transpires with absolutely everything. Otherwise, why would He have created something; because He was bored?

Whenever we have anything to eat, we have an opportunity not only to taste something delicious, but also, in a sense, to "taste" the presence of God's will in all creation. When we make a blessing, we become aware that we are about to partake of a precious bit of God's creation—a spark of holiness—and we pray that we will use that morsel of Divine will to fulfill our highest personal potential.

Myths & Facts

Myth: Kosher food is bland, brown, and salty.

Fact: There is no reason in the world why kosher food can't be knock-your-socks-off delicious. Keeping kosher never stood in the way of anyone cooking great looking and great tasting food.

Susie Fishbein is the best-selling author of the *Kosher by Design* cookbook series (ArtScroll/Mesorah Publications, Ltd. © 2003, 2005), and Scott Sunshine regularly caters events such as the Masters Golf Tournament, the U.S. Open Tennis Championship, and the Super Bowl. He has also been called upon to prepare a tea reception for the First Lady. These two chefs have prepared some wonderful recipes for you. Please enjoy this cookbook, and more importantly, enjoy some great kosher cooking.

CONTENTS

new-age shish kebobs meat

Courtesy of Chef Scott Sunshine

4 medium chicken legs
  boned
1 large green bell pepper
8 tablespoons Shoya or
  light soy sauce
4 tablespoons sake or
  dry sherry
3 tablespoons sugar

1. Cut both the chicken and pepper into 1-inch cubes. Thread them onto the skewers by alternating two pieces of chicken with one piece of pepper. Leave at least 1 inch of space at each end. Cover with plastic wrap and refrigerate until needed.

2. Combine the soy sauce, sake, and sugar in a small pan and bring it to a boil. Lower the heat and stir gently until the sugar has dissolved.

3. Preheat an indoor broiler or an outdoor charcoal grill. Position the skewers 4-5 inches from the heat source, and grill them 4-5 minutes on each side or until the meat is 3/4 cooked. Brush the shish kebobs with the sauce and grill briefly on both sides until the meat is almost done. Brush them with the sauce one last time and grill them for another 30 seconds on each side. Serve hot.

Yield: 4 servings

tri-color gefilte fish pareve

Kosher by Design © 2003
This easy spin on traditional gefilte fish has three different colored layers for a sophisticated look. It takes only 5 minutes to prepare. The recipe is based on a 9-inch springform pan with a removable bottom. If you are using a larger springform pan you may need to use 1-2 loaves per layer. Playing with the amounts won't affect the cooking method, but you may need to increase the cooking time by 10-15 minutes.

2 (22-ounce) loaves plain gefilte
fish, defrosted in wrapper
1 (22-ounce) loaf salmon gefilte
fish, defrosted in wrapper
2 tablespoons fresh dill, chopped
1 lemon
6 cucumbers for horseradish
wells, plus one extra long
cucumber for top garnish
(optional)
prepared red horseradish
(optional)
mayonnaise (optional)
yellow pepper (optional)

1. Preheat oven to 350 degrees. Spray a 9-inch springform pan with nonstick vegetable spray. Give it a heavy even coat. Open each of the 3 gefilte fish wrappers.

2. Add the dill and juice from lemon into one of the plain gefilte fish loaves. Mix thoroughly so the dill is dispersed evenly. Set aside.

3. Using a thin spatula, spread the plain gefilte fish into an even layer in the bottom of the springform pan. Top with an even layer of the salmon. On top of the salmon, spread an even layer of the lemon dill fish mixture.

4. Cover the pan with foil. Bake for 1 hour. If the fish does not look set in the center, remove the foil and bake 5 minutes longer.

5. Let cool and refrigerate overnight. Can be made a few days in advance. As an optional garnish, slice a long unpeeled cucumber by hand or by mandoline into paper thin slices. Lay the slices in concentric circles around the top of the fish.

6. Release the sides of the springform pan. To serve as individual servings, cut into wedges, like a pie. Trim any brown edges.

7. Cut the cucumbers into 2- to 3-inch pieces. Hollow out the center. Mix a few tablespoons of the prepared horseradish with a little mayonnaise to make a pretty pink sauce. Fill the cucumber wells.

8. Serve a slice of fish on a piece of leafy lettuce with a cucumber well. You can decorate each plate with tiny squares of yellow pepper.

Yield: 10-12 servings

two-tone sweet pea & carrot soup
meat or pareve

Kosher by Design © 2003

Either soup can be made on its own, but the colors and flavors of this two-toned combination are fabulous. Try serving the soup in half a baby pumpkin if the season is right. Have the produce department halve the pumpkins for you; they can be difficult to cut. This pea soup is very different from split-pea soup, which most people are used to. It is thin, smooth, and a gorgeous green.

Carrot Soup:

6   cups vegetable or chicken stock or bouillon dissolved in water
7   tablespoons margarine, divided
4   tablespoons all-purpose flour

1   large onion, chopped
1   leek, white and light green parts thinly sliced, discarding the rest
2   pounds carrots, peeled and cut into chunks

Green Pea Soup:

6   cups vegetable or chicken stock or bouillon dissolved in water
7   tablespoons margarine, divided
4   tablespoons all-purpose flour
1   large onion, chopped

1   leek, white and light green parts only, thinly sliced
1   (20-ounce) bag frozen green peas

1. Bring the stock or bouillon to a boil. Reduce heat and simmer to keep warm.

2. To make either the carrot or sweet pea soup: Prepare a roux. In a large pot, heat four tablespoons of the margarine over low heat. Add the flour, whisking until smooth. Cook for 1 minute, whisking constantly. It will thicken. Add 1 tablespoon of margarine. Add the onion and leek; sauté 5-7 minutes or until translucent.

3. Add remaining 2 tablespoons margarine to the pot. Add vegetables (either the carrots or the peas). Sauté about 5-10 minutes; the carrots will take longer.

4. Stir hot stock into the vegetables. Bring mixture to a boil; reduce heat. Simmer, covered, 30 minutes.   ▶▶

5. Transfer soup in batches to the container of a blender; process until smooth. You may also use an immersion blender right in the pot. If the carrot soup is too thick, thin with a little stock, soy milk, or nondairy creamer. The pea soup must be poured through a strainer to get all of the shells out; press with back of a spoon to release all of the liquid.

Yield: 6 servings of single vegetable batch; 10-12 servings of two-tone batch

wild mushroom velouté soup
meat, pareve, or dairy

Kosher by Design Entertains © 2005

A velouté is a thickened soup, similar to a bisque. It is quick cooking and so simple to prepare. In some markets, the wild mushrooms are packaged together. You can just buy 18-20 ounces total of the assorted packages.

I love the covered crocks pictured here. I use them often for soups and stews but my favorite use is for serving individual portions of cholent on Shabbos.

2 tablespoons olive oil
1 cup (about 4 ounces) sliced shiitake mushroom, stems discarded
2 cups (6-7 ounces) sliced oyster mushrooms
2 cups (6-7 ounces) sliced cremini mushrooms
2 cloves garlic, chopped

1 small onion, cut into small dice
⅛ teaspoon dried thyme
8 tablespoons margarine or butter
½ cup all-purpose flour
7 cups chicken or vegetable broth, warm
⅛ teaspoon sea salt
⅛ teaspoon freshly ground black pepper

1. Heat oil in medium pot over medium heat. Add the mushrooms and sauté until tender, about 4 minutes. Add in the garlic and onion. Cook for 4-5 minutes. Sprinkle in the thyme. Add the margarine or butter and melt. Slowly sprinkle in the flour. The mixture will form a sticky mixture called a roux. Slowly add the stock and simmer, uncovered, for 20 minutes to cook out the floury taste.

2. Season with salt and pepper.

Yield: 8 servings

zahara's gazpacho pareve

Courtesy of Chef Scott Sunshine

1 cup red onion, chopped	1/4 cup tomato paste
1 cup green pepper, chopped	1 tablespoon white wine vinegar
1 cup English cucumber. chopped	1/4 cup plus 2 tablespoons extra virgin
1 cup tomatoes, peeled and chopped	olive oil
1/2 teaspoons fresh garlic, chopped	1 tablespoon fresh lemon juice
1/2 teaspoons kosher salt	3 cups tomato juice
1/4 teaspoon cayenne	sprig of thyme

MARTY KATZ PHOTOGRAPHY

1. Mix all the ingredients together. Cover and let them sit in the refrigerator overnight.

2. Remove the thyme from the vegetable mixture. Place all the other ingredients in a blender, and blend them until smooth. If you want your gazpacho to be really smooth, you may also strain it through a sieve in order to remove the vegetable chunks and pulp.

3. Refrigerate the gazpacho until ready to serve.

Yield: Approximately 2 quarts

candied almond, pear, and goat cheese salad with shallot vinaigrette dairy

Kosher by Design © 2003

Right now it is difficult to find Kosher bleu or gorgonzola cheese. But it is produced Kosher in Denmark, so there is a chance it will be available in the United States soon. In the meantime goat cheese works very well.

Vinaigrette:

2	tablespoons balsamic vinegar	1/4	cup plus 2 tablespoons good quality olive oil
1	teaspoon minced shallot		salt & freshly ground black pepper

Candied Almonds:

1 1/2	cups slivered almonds	2/3	cup sugar

Salad:

5	cups mesclun mix	1/2	cup sweetened dried cranberries
2	cups arugula, torn	1 1/2	ounces goat cheese, bleu cheese, or gorgonzola, crumbled
2	pears, cored and cubed		salt & freshly ground black pepper
1	cup red grapes, halved		

Vinaigrette:

Place the vinegar, shallot, olive oil, salt, and pepper in a jar or cruet. Shake until emulsified. Set aside.

Candied Almonds:

1. Cover a baking sheet with tin foil. In a nonstick skillet sprayed with nonstick cooking spray, heat the almonds over medium heat. Cook 2-3 minutes to toast the almonds, gently shaking the skillet.

2. Slowly add the sugar; cook about 8-9 minutes, stirring constantly, to keep the almonds separated as the sugar caramelizes. The sugar will turn a deep amber color; make sure not to burn the sugar.

3. Remove from heat immediately and quickly spread the almonds onto the prepared baking sheet. Separate them to prevent clumping. If making the almonds in advance keep them in an airtight container.

Salad:

In a large bowl toss the mesclun, arugula, pears, grapes, cranberries, and cheese. Sprinkle over the candied almonds and coat with the vinaigrette. Season with salt and pepper to taste.

Yield: 6 servings

carrot muffins pareve

Kosher by Design: Kids in the Kitchen © 2005

My mom used to make these all the time when I was growing up. They were always a hit with me and my friends.

1   cup sugar
1   cup all-purpose flour
3/4 cup canola oil
12 ounces baby food carrots
    (usually 3 jars)
1   teaspoon baking soda
1   teaspoon cinnamon
2   large eggs

1. Preheat the oven to 350° F.

2. Place the sugar, flour, and oil into a medium mixing bowl. Add the baby food carrots, using your small spatula or a spoon to get all of the baby food out of the jar.

3. Add the baking soda, cinnamon, and eggs.

4. Mix with an electric mixer at medium speed for 3 minutes, until the batter is smooth.

5. Place the paper muffin cups into a muffin or cupcake tray.

6. If your measuring cup has a spout, pour the batter from the measuring cup into the muffin cups; if not, use a large spoon. Fill the muffin cups almost to the top.

7. Place tray into the oven and bake for 30 minutes.

8. Open the oven and carefully pull out the muffin tray. Stick a toothpick into the center of a muffin; it should come out clean. If is comes out gooey, return the muffins to the oven for another 2-3 minutes. When the muffins are done, remove from the oven and allow the muffins to cool.

Yield: 12-14 muffins

chicken salad with grapes and walnuts meat

Courtesy of Chef Scott Sunshine

4 cups cooked chicken, cubed
1 cup walnuts, toasted and chopped
1 celery rib, cut into 1/4 - inch-thick slices
2 tablespoons shallot, chopped finely
2 cups seedless red grapes, halved
3/4 cup mayonnaise
3 tablespoons tarragon vinegar
2 tablespoons fresh tarragon, chopped finely
1/2 teaspoon salt
1/2 teaspoon black pepper

MARTY KATZ PHOTOGRAPHY

In a large bowl, toss all ingredients together until they are combined well.

Yield: 4-6 servings

hearty root vegetable ragout meat

Courtesy of Chef Scott Sunshine

1/2 pound pearl onions (about 1 cup)
1 medium turnip
1 medium Yukon Gold
2 medium carrots

2 medium parsnips
2 teaspoons vegetable oil
2 tablespoons unsalted margarine
1/2 cup beef stock

1. Preheat oven to 425°F. Have ready a bowl of ice and cold water.

2. Cook the onions in boiling water for 3 minutes and drain them in a colander. Transfer the onions to the ice water to stop the cooking. When the onions are cool enough to handle, peel them and set them aside. Peel the remaining vegetables and cut them into 1/2-inch cubes. In a shallow roasting pan, toss the vegetables (except onions) with oil and roast them in the middle of the oven until tender and golden, about 20 minutes.

3. In a large skillet, heat the margarine over a moderate heat, and cook the onions until they are tender and lightly browned. Add the roasted vegetables, stock, salt, and pepper, and simmer them for about 2 minutes, or until the stock is slightly thickened and coats the vegetables.

Yield: 4 servings

jewel-toned orzo pareve or meat

Kosher by Design Entertains © 2005

2 tablespoons margarine	1/2 cup sweetened dried cranberries
2 large onions, cut into 1/4-inch dice	1/4 teaspoon sea salt
1 green bell pepper, seeded and cut into 1/4-inch dice	1/4 teaspoon ground white pepper
1 yellow bell pepper, seeded and cut into 1/4-inch dice	1 tablespoon canola oil
	1 (16-ounce) box orzo
8 ounces fresh sliced mushrooms	1 1/2 teaspoons chicken bouillon powder (can be pareve)

1. In a large pan, over medium heat, melt the margarine. Add the onions, peppers, mushrooms, and cranberries. Sauté until softened, about 6-8 minutes, making sure not to let the vegetables brown or burn. Season with the salt and white pepper. Set aside.

2. Meanwhile, in a medium pot, heat the oil. Add the orzo and toast until golden, stirring often. It will be all different shades of brown and have a nutty aroma. Add boiling water to cover by a few inches and the bouillon powder. Cook until the orzo is al denté, about 8-9 minutes. If the water boils out and the orzo is still too hard, add more hot water 1/2 cup at a time, stirring to make sure the orzo is not sticking to the bottom of the pot, until orzo is done and water has evaporated.

3. Combine the vegetables with the orzo. Serve hot or at room temperature.

Yield: 8-10 servings

roasted beets and baby greens with coriander vinaigrette and cilantro pesto pareve

Courtesy of Chef Scott Sunshine

Vinaigrette

| 1 | tablespoon whole coriander seeds
| 1/2 | cup extra virgin olive oil, divided
| 1/4 | cup shallots, minced
| 2 | tablespoons balsamic vinegar

| 1 | small garlic clove, peeled
| 1/2 | teaspoon coarse kosher salt
| 1/2 | teaspoon freshly ground black pepper

Pesto

| 1 | cup extra virgin olive oil
| 1/2 | cup pine nuts, toasted
| 1 | bunch fresh cilantro, coarsely chopped (about 2 cups)
| 1 | bunch fresh chives, coarsely chopped (about 1/3 cup)
| 1/4 | cup (packed) fresh mint leaves

| 1 | tablespoon seeded jalapeño chile, chopped
| 1 | small garlic clove, peeled
| 1 | teaspoon (scant) coarse kosher salt
| 1/2 | teaspoon freshly ground black pepper
| 3 | tablespoons fresh lime juice

MARTY KATZ PHOTOGRAPHY

Beets

| 1 | pound yellow beets
| 1 | pound red baby beets
| 1 | tablespoon olive oil
| | Coarse kosher salt

Greens

| 6 | cups assorted red baby lettuces (such as red oak leaf and lolla rossa) coarse kosher salt

►►

For Vinaigrette:

1. Place the coriander in a small skillet over a medium heat. While stirring continuously, cook the coriander until it is fragrant, about 4 minutes. Cool, then coarsely grind the coriander in a spice mill or with a mortar and pestle. Transfer it to a small bowl.

2. Over a medium heat, place 1 tablespoon of the oil into the same skillet that you just used for the coriander. Add the shallots, and saute them for about 3 minutes or until they are soft. Combine them with the coriander, and then add the vinegar, garlic, salt, and pepper. Gradually whisk in the remaining 7 tablespoons of oil. *Note:* If you are making this in advance, be sure to cover and chill the vinaigrette at this point. Discard the garlic after 1 hour, and allow the vinaigrette to stand at room temperature for 1 hour before serving.

For Pesto:

1. Puree the first 9 ingredients in a blender until they are smooth.

2. Whisk in the lime juice.

For Beets:

1. Preheat oven to 350°F. Wash and dry the beets, then cut off the beet greens one inch from the top of the beets.

2. Rub the beets with oil. Place the yellow beets in one roasting pan and the red beets in another; sprinkle them with coarse salt. Cover the pans tightly with foil, and roast the beets for about 55 minutes or until they are tender. Cool slightly.

3. Using a towel, rub off the peel and stems from beets. Cut the beets in half, and place the yellow and red beets in two separate bowls. Toss the beets in each bowl with 2 tablespoons of the vinaigrette. Let them stand for about 30 minutes.

Salad Assembly:

Combine and toss the lettuce with enough vinaigrette to coat it lightly. Divide the lettuce among the plates and top each serving with the beets. Drizzle pesto over all.

Yield: 4-6 servings

braised beef short ribs meat

*Courtesy of
Chef Scott Sunshine*

1	small onion
1	medium carrot
1/4	cup plus 1 tablespoon vegetable oil
1	cup dry red wine
3	thyme sprigs
1	bay leaf
1/2	teaspoon cracked black pepper
4	(3/4 lb.) beef short ribs or flanken all-purpose flour for dusting ribs
2	cups beef stock, plus1/2 cup water (if necessary)

MARTY KATZ PHOTOGRAPHY

Pictured here with Hearty Root Vegetable Ragout, page 127.

1. Slice the onion and chop the carrot. Over moderate heat, cook the vegetables in 1 tablespoon oil for 2-3 minutes, or until soft but not browned. Add the wine, thyme, bay leaf, and pepper. Simmer for 3 minutes. Transfer the mixture to a bowl to cool.

2. In a heavy-duty sealable plastic bag, combine the ribs and wine mixture. Place the bag in the refrigerator, and marinate for at least 8 hours, turning occasionally.

3. Preheat oven to 300°F. Remove the ribs from the marinade and pat them dry. Pour the marinade through a sieve and into a small saucepan. Discard the solids. Bring the marinade to a boil, skimming the froth, and remove the pan from the heat.

4. Season the ribs well with salt and pepper and lightly dust them with flour. In a heavy ovenproof skillet, heat the remaining 1/4 cup oil over a moderately high heat until it just begins to give off a faint white smoke. Brown the ribs, turning them occasionally, and transfer them to a plate.

5. Pour off the oil from the skillet and add the ribs and stock. Pour the marinade into the skillet and bring the liquid to a simmer. Cover the skillet with foil or a lid, and braise the ribs in the middle of the oven for 4 hours or until meat gives no resistance when pierced with a fork (add water after 3 hours if most of braising liquid has evaporated). Through a sieve, pour braising liquid into a bowl and skim the fat.

Yield: 4 servings

chicken shiraz with mushrooms and shallots meat

MARTY KATZ PHOTOGRAPHY

Courtesy of
Chef Scott Sunshine

2   cups chicken stock
1   ounce dried porcini
    mushrooms
1   teaspoon olive oil
4   large chicken breast
    halves with skin and
    bones, each cut cross-
    wise in half
3   chicken thighs with
    skin and bones

3   chicken drumsticks with skin and
    bones
6   whole shallots
10 ounces crimini (baby bella)
    mushrooms, halved
1/3 cup shallots, chopped

2   teaspoons fresh thyme, chopped
2   garlic cloves, chopped
1/4 cup all purpose flour
2   cups Shiraz or other hearty red wine
    fresh Italian parsley, chopped

1. Preheat oven to 300°F. Bring broth and porcini mushrooms to boil in small saucepan. Remove from heat and let stand at room temperature until mushrooms soften, about 25 minutes. Using slotted spoon, transfer mushrooms to cutting board and chop coarsely. Pour mushroom broth into medium bowl, leaving sediment behind. Reserve broth.

2. Meanwhile, heat oil in heavy large ovenproof pot over medium heat. Sprinkle all chicken pieces with salt and pepper. Working in batches, add chicken to pot and cook over medium-high heat until lightly browned, about 5 minutes per side. Transfer chicken to platter.

3. Pour off all but 3 tablespoons chicken drippings from pot. Add whole shallots to pot, and cook until lightly browned, about 2 minutes per side. Add crimini mushrooms. Cook until mushrooms begin to brown, stirring frequently, for about 6 minutes. Stir in chopped shallots, thyme, garlic, and reserved porcini mushrooms; cook until chopped shallots are soft, about 2 minutes. Stir flour into shallot mixture and continue stirring 1 minute. Stir in wine and reserved mushroom broth, then add chicken thighs and drumsticks to pot. Bring to boil.

4. Cover pot and transfer to oven. Bake 25 minutes. Add chicken breasts to pot. Cover and bake until all chicken is cooked through, about 45 minutes longer. Using

▶▶

slotted spoon, transfer chicken to platter; tent with foil to keep warm.

5. Boil sauce in pot until slightly thickened, about 5 minutes. Pour sauce over chicken on platter, sprinkle with parsley, and serve.

Yield: 4-6 servings

eggplant with marinated tofu, caramelized red onion, and fennel pareve

Courtesy of Chef Scott Sunshine

This dish may be served warm or cold as a salad or entrée.

1	large eggplant	1	large bulb fennel
1	block extra firm tofu		extra virgin olive oil
2	medium red onions		spicy paprika
1	medium head Freisse or	3/4	cup balsamic vinegar
	other bitter green	1/4	cup toasted sesame oil

1. Cut the tofu into solid 1/4 inch rectangles. Place them in a bowl, and cover them with a mixture of the balsamic vinegar and toasted sesame oil. Allow marinade to penetrate the tofu (1-2 hours), and then set them aside until assembly time.

2. Cut the onion in half and then slice thinly. Heat heavy sauté pan with 3 tablespoons of olive oil. Add onions and cook over medium heat. Stir regularly until onions caramelize. This means that they will be soft and slightly browned from the released sugars.

3. Remove the root end and feathery top from the fennel. Reserve the top for garnish. Slice the fennel in half and then into thin slices. Heat heavy sauté pan with 6 tablespoons of olive oil. Add fennel and cook over medium heat. Stir regularly until fennel caramelizes.

4. Preheat oven to 350°F. Cut the eggplant into 1/2 inch round slices. Arrange them on a baking sheet and sprinkle with olive oil and paprika. Bake about 10 minutes or until soft.

5. Clean greens and separate them into small bunches. Place an eggplant slice on a plate, followed by a spoon of onion, then eggplant, greens, eggplant, tofu, eggplant, and fennel. Drizzle with the balsamic mixture and garnish with the fennel tops.

Yield: 6 servings as a salad or 4 servings as an entrée

spinach linguine with walnut cream sauce dairy

Kosher by Design Entertains © 2005

1   pound spinach linguine or
    spinach fettuccine
2   cups walnut halves
1   cup heavy cream
1/2 cup fresh baby spinach
    leaves, minced
1   clove garlic, minced
    salt
    freshly ground black pepper
1/4 cup grated Parmesan
    fresh parsley, chopped for
    garnish

1. Preheat oven to 350° F.

2. Cook pasta; when ready, drain and set aside.

3. While pasta is cooking, spread the walnuts on a parchment lined baking sheet; toast for 8-10 minutes until fragrant. Remove from oven.

4. Place 1 cup of the walnut halves into the bowl of a food processor fitted with a metal blade and process until finely chopped but not ground. Transfer to a large pot. Add the cream, spinach, and garlic. Place over low heat and bring to a simmer. Add in the cooked pasta and toss to coat. Mix in the remaining cup of walnuts, reserving a few for garnish. Season with salt and pepper.

5. Remove to a platter or bowl. Sprinkle with the Parmesan and chopped parsley. Garnish with reserved walnut halves.

Yield: 6 servings

tuna steaks with white beans and sun-dried tomato sauce pareve

Courtesy of Chef Scott Sunshine

1   cup dried Great Northern beans
5   cups chicken stock
7   tablespoons olive oil
1/2 cup onion, chopped
1/2 cup carrot, chopped

1/2 cup celery, chopped
5   teaspoons fresh thyme, chopped, or
    2 teaspoons dried
1   tablespoon lemon peel, grated
4   (6-8 oz.) ahi tuna steaks (each
    about 3/4"- 1" thick)

▶▶

Sun-Dried Tomato Sauce

¹/₂	cup oil-packed sun-dried tomatoes, drained	I	cup non-dairy creamer or soy milk	
I	cup dry white wine	I	tablespoon corn starch	
¹/₄	cup white wine vinegar	¹/₂	cup chicken stock	
10	black peppercorns	I	tablespoon fresh thyme, minced, or 1 teaspoon dried	
I	bay leaf			

Preparing the Tuna Steaks with White Beans

1. Place the beans in a medium bowl. Add enough cold water to cover the beans by 3 inches. Let them stand overnight and then drain them.

MARTY KATZ PHOTOGRAPHY

2. Combine the beans and stock in a large saucepan. Bring them to a boil, reduce the heat to medium, and then cover and simmer for about an hour or until the beans are tender. Drain and reserve 1/2 cup of the cooking liquid.

3. Heat 3 tablespoons of oil in a heavy, large skillet over a medium heat. Add the onion, carrot, and celery, and saute for about 5 minutes or until almost tender. Add the thyme and lemon peel and stir them for about 1 minute. Add the beans, the reserved cooking liquid, and 2 tablespoons of oil. Toss until heated through, and then season to taste with salt and pepper.

4. Remove from heat. Cover to keep warm.

5. Heat the remaining 2 tablespoons of oil in another large skillet over a medium-high heat. Sprinkle the tuna with salt and pepper, then add them to the skillet and cook to desired doneness (about 3 minutes per side for medium).

Sun-Dried Tomato Sauce

1. Place the sun-dried tomatoes in a food processor. Boil the wine, vinegar, black peppercorns, and bay leaf in a small pan for 8 minutes or until the liquid is reduced

▶▶

to 3 tablespoons. Strain the liquid into the tomatoes, and place them both in the food processor. Pureé them until they are smooth. Return pureé to the saucepan.

2. In a separate cup or bowl, mix the corn starch with the cold non-dairy creamer or soy milk. Once the corn starch has dissolved, add it to the mixture in the saucepan, and then add the chicken stock and thyme. Simmer for about 3 minutes or until the flavors blend together. Season to taste with salt.

Yield: 4 servings

baked apples with cranberries, raisins, and apricots pareve

Courtesy of Chef Scott Sunshine

4	large Fuji apples
1/2	cup golden raisins
1/2	cup dried cranberries
1/3	cup packed brown sugar
1/4	cup dried apricots, chopped
3/4	teaspoon ground allspice, divided
1/4	cup unsalted margarine, melted
2	cups apple-cranberry juice
1/4	cup frozen concentrated cranberry juice cocktail, thawed

MARTY KATZ PHOTOGRAPHY

1. Preheat oven to 400°F. Remove the stems from the apples. Using a corer, scoop out the core of each apple, making a 1"-wide hollow center but leaving the bottom of the apple intact.

2. Make a 1/8"-deep cut in the skin around the center of each apple. Arrange the apples, hollowed side up, in an 8 x 8 x 2 glass baking dish.

3. Mix the raisins, cranberries, sugar, apricots, and 1/2 teaspoon allspice in a small bowl. Pack the fruit mixture into the hollows of the apples. Sprinkle any remaining fruit mixture around the apples in the dish. Drizzle the margarine over the filling

▶▶

and apples, pour the apple-cranberry juice into the dish, and then sprinkle the remaining 1/2 teaspoon allspice over the entire dish contents.

4. Bake the apples uncovered for about 1 hour and 10 minutes, or until tender, and be sure to occasionally baste them with the cranberry juice mixture.

5. Transfer the apples to 4 bowls. Pour the juices from the dish into a medium saucepan, and boil them for about 4 minutes, or until they are thick enough to coat a spoon.

6. Spoon the sauce over apples.

Yield: 4 servings

blueberry lemon crème brûlée tart

pareve or dairy

Kosher by Design Entertains © 2005

Crust:

13	tablespoons unsalted butter or margarine, at room temperature for 15 minutes
1/3	cup confectioner's sugar
1	large egg yolk
1 1/2	cups unbleached all-purpose flour
1	tablespoon heavy cream or soy milk
1	egg white, whisked, for brushing after tart is baked

Blueberry Lemon Filling:

1	cup sugar
	grated zest of 1 lemon, preferably a Meyer lemon
1/2	cup freshly squeezed lemon juice, about 4-5 lemons worth
1	large egg yolk
4	large eggs
3/4	cup heavy cream or soy milk
3	tablespoons unsalted butter or margarine, melted
1/2	cup fresh blueberries
2-3	tablespoons sugar

▶▶

1. Place the butter or margarine and the confectioner's sugar into the bowl of a stand mixer. Cream the mixture at medium speed until no sugar is visible. Scrape down the sides of the bowl with a spatula. Add the egg yolk and beat until blended. Scrape down the sides of the bowl again. Add half of the flour and beat until dough becomes crumbly. Add remaining flour and the cream or soy milk. Beat until dough forms a sticky mass. Scrape the dough onto a piece of parchment or waxed paper. Flatten into a disc and place in refrigerator until firm, about 2 hours.

2. Remove from the refrigerator and press into the bottom and up the sides of a 10-inch tart pan with removable bottom. The dough will be sticky, so don't bother with a rolling pin. Just flour your hands and use the heel of your palm and the side of your thumb to work it evenly into the pan. Place this shell into the freezer for 30 minutes.

3. Preheat oven to 375° F. Prick the bottom of the tart all over with a fork. Place tart pan on a baking sheet; the heat it conducts will help brown the crust evenly. Bake the tart shell for 18-20 minutes, until pastry is golden and the interior is dry. Remove tart from oven and evenly brush the egg white over the entire surface of the tart. Reduce oven temperature to 350° F.

4. Prepare the filling. Place the sugar and lemon zest into a medium bowl. Rub the sugar and zest together between the palms of your hands. Add the lemon juice, egg yolk, eggs, cream or soy milk, and melted butter or margarine. Whisk to combine. Pour filling into crust. Sprinkle in the fresh blueberries, scattering them evenly in the tart filling. Bake until filling is slightly puffed at edges and set in center, about 30 minutes. Cool completely, about 1 hour.

5. If you have a hand held blow torch, it is a snap to caramelize the top. Sprinkle the sugar evenly over the tart, then with the torch nozzle 4 inches from the top, circle the flame until the sugar has melted and caramelizes. If you don't have a torch, preheat the oven to broil. Carefully wrap the exposed tart dough with aluminum foil, or it will turn black. Place the tart on a rack 4-6 inches from broiler coil. Sprinkle the sugar evenly over the filling. Place under the broiler from 2-5 minutes, watching the entire time to make sure the sugar turns golden brown and caramelized but doesn't burn. Turn the pan for even browning.

6. Store at room temperature.

Yield: 10-12 servings

citrus granita pareve

Courtesy of Chef Scott Sunshine

This dish is cool and refreshing. It may be made with almost any fruit, but those with a higher acid content give it a lovely crispness.

4 medium grapefruits or other citrus fruit	$^2/_3$ cup sugar 2 cups water

MARTY KATZ PHOTOGRAPHY

1. Zest the grapefruit – try to get long strips. Squeeze at least 1/2 cup of juice from the grapefruit.

2. In a small, heavy saucepan, heat the water, dissolve the sugar, and stir in the zest. Simmer for 15 minutes. Transfer into a bowl to cool; chill until cold, remove the zest, and then stir in the juice.

3. Freeze the mix in a metal bowl, giving a stir every 30 minutes to remove the ice from the sides of the bowl. Continue to do this until the mix is granular but still slightly slushy, about 3-4 hours. You may serve this immediately, but if you're not ready, you may continuously scrape up the mixture to reestablish the grainy texture.

Yield: 4 servings

marble fudge cookie pareve

Kosher by Design © 2003

Many of you will recognize these as Chinese cookies. Taste these and you'll agree that these melt-in-your-mouth, puddle-of-fudge delights deserved a better name.

Cookies:

- 3 cups all-purpose flour
- 1 1/2 cups pure vegetable shortening, like Crisco (no substitutes)
- 1 1/2 cups sugar
- 1 1/4 teaspoons baking soda
- 1 large egg
- 1/4 cup chocolate chips (about 1 ounce)

Fudge Glaze:

- 6 ounces chocolate chips
- 3 tablespoons vegetable shortening
- 1 tablespoon confectioner's sugar

Cookies:

1. In a large mixing bowl, with mixer at medium speed, mix the flour, shortening, sugar, and baking soda. Add the egg. Mix until dough forms.

2. Place the chocolate chips in a glass bowl and melt in the microwave for 1 minute at 70%; stir to hasten melting. With a knife, cut the melted chocolate into the dough, swirling as best you can.

3. Using parchment or waxed paper, roll the dough into 3 logs, each about the size of a salami or 2 1/2 - 3-inch in diameter. Freeze for 1/2 hour -1 hour to make the slicing neater and easier.

4. Preheat oven to 350°. Spray 2 cookie sheets with nonstick cooking spray or line with parchment paper. Slice each log into 12-15 cookies. Bake 15-20 minutes. Let cool on a rack.

Glaze:

Either in a double boiler or in the microwave, melt the chocolate chips with the shortening and confectioner's sugar. Stir till smooth and shiny. Put a puddle in the center of each cookie. Place in refrigerator for 10 minutes to set the chocolate. Store in a single layer so chocolate doesn't smudge. Alternatively, for the centers you can use 8 ounces of melted Shufra baking chocolate, puddled in the center of each cookie.

Yield: 30-34 cookies

poached pears with chocolate sauce
dairy or pareve

MARTY KATZ PHOTOGRAPHY

*Courtesy of Chef
Scott Sunshine*

*May be served warm
or cold.*

1   cup dark brown sugar
4   tablespoons dark rum
4   large pears
2   ounces bittersweet
    chocolate, chopped
4   tablespoons vanilla
    extract
1   cup plus another 1/2 cup
    water

1. Peel the pears and cut a small amount off the bottoms so that the fruit will stand up straight.

2. In a heavy saucepan, combine the rum and sugar with 1 cup of water, and cook them for three minutes. Add the pears and poach them for about 15 minutes or until they are tender. While they are poaching, be sure to continuously spoon the liquid over the fruit.

3. In a second pot, combine the remaining 1/2 cup of water with the vanilla extract and chocolate, and stir until smooth.

4. Stand each pear on a plate and drizzle the chocolate sauce over it.

Yield: 4 servings

The World Wide *Kosher* Web

There is an urban legend that the World Wide Web was created by two Jewish ladies who wanted to market their kosher strudel and rugelach to Jews around the world. Like most urban legends, it's not true.

Legends aside, the Internet has been as much a boon for the kosher consumer as it has for anyone else. Two examples: A neighbor of mine sells a variety of challahs and delicious homemade baked goods at **www.rachaelsgourmetdelectables.com.** Another neighbor recently opened a great kosher candy store in Baltimore where she sells fantastic gift baskets and other goodies at **www.thecandystoreonline.com.**

www.thecandystoreonline.com

www.thecandystoreonline.com

Today, if you want dynamite kosher desserts, you don't have to *shlepp* to New York — you can just log on to **www.kosher.com** and order to your heart's delight. If you live in Indianapolis, Birmingham, or Sioux City, and you have a craving for kosher pizza, just surf the web and twenty-four hours later you will have your pizza.

The following is a small sampling of web sites that that have great products for both the kosher palate and the kosher chef.

B'tayavon – bon appétit!

Note: *As a kosher consumer, it is important that you be as careful when shopping on-line as you are when shopping at the grocery store. Please make sure there is reliable kosher supervision for all the products you purchase.*

www.aish.com/family/cooking
www.challahconnection.com
www.flyingpizzas.com
www.igourmet.com
www.kosherbison.com

www.kosheritalia.com
www.koshermealstogo.com
www.kosherwine.com
www.thekosherconnection.com
www.thekoshercook.com

Chapter 5
If I Kosher My Kitchen, Do I Have to Paint It Too?

Let's be perfectly honest, you have just decided to make a huge change in your life, and change is never easy. The truth is, you are in for some short-term stress, but before you know it you will have successfully launched a wonderful new chapter in your life, and you can be proud of that.

The Jewish story is a story that spans three millennia. As a Jew, you are part of a people—a history and an odyssey—that has been unfolding for hundreds of generations, that is as alive and vibrant today as it has ever been, and that has a brilliant future. Without a doubt, the kosher home and the kosher kitchen have always been, and always will be, central elements to the Jewish story. And now, as a result of your decision to kasher your home, you are about to become more profoundly rooted in the story of your people than ever before. Mazel tov!

DON'T TRY THIS ON YOUR OWN

Almost everyone who goes through the process of beginning to keep kosher does so with at least some help from a rabbi or knowledgeable friend. Now that you have decided to take the kosher kitchen plunge, it is absolutely critical that you be assisted by someone who knows what he or she is doing. You can think of this person as your personal kashering coach. This is not the time for exercising your do-it-yourself muscle for at least three reasons.

1. A whole area of intricate Jewish law applies to kashering a home, and if you don't know the rules, you may end up doing lots and lots of work and not having a kosher kitchen to show for it.

2. Your spiritual well-being depends on doing this correctly, and if you have a family, so does theirs. So you want to make sure that the deep Jewish commitment you are making leads to the deep Jewish results you have in mind.

3. You want your "kosher" friends to feel perfectly comfortable as guests in your home. If someone who genuinely knows halacha (Jewish law) guides you through the process, then others can be confident that the food they are served in your home is 100 percent kosher. If you attempt to kasher your kitchen on your own, you will inevitably put others and yourself in an awkward situation. And that's the last thing you want to do.

So, bottom line, you've just got to do this thing right, and doing it right means making sure you've got an expert at your side. (If you don't know whom to contact, send me an e-mail at shimon@leviathanpress.com and I'll be happy to help you track down someone in your area.)

FIVE AND A HALF STEPS TO A KOSHER KITCHEN

wise man once said, "look before you leap," and that is certainly good advice when it comes to kashering your home. Before we get into the nitty-gritty, we'll take a look at an overview of the five-and-a-half-step-process that you are about to embark upon.

One of the great tragedies of our time is how desensitized we have become to human suffering. Anything less than a tsunami and we just flip to the next item in the newspaper. Sensitivity creates empathy, connection, and relationship. Insensitivity creates distance and dissonance. In our spiritual lives, the more sensitive and attuned we become to our souls and to the presence of God that permeates creation, the deeper is our potential for closeness to God. The Talmud teaches that the consumption of nonkosher foods makes it harder for us to detect spiritual moments, to be attuned to the longing of our souls, and to connect with the deepest dimensions of life.

And now for a brief explanation of what to expect during each one of these steps in the process.

- **Step 1**—Crate and Barrel: This is probably the most painful part of the process for the simple reason that it hits you where it hurts—in the checkbook. The good news, however, is that the majority of items in your kitchen can be either kashered or, better yet, just cleaned. In this step, you will take a tour of your kitchen with someone who is well-versed in the laws of kashering a kitchen. You will need to examine your cookware, cutlery, and other kitchen utensils to determine which can be made kosher and which can't. Once you know what can be kashered you will have a good sense of two things: how much work the kashering process will involve and how much you are going to have to spend on new items. Usually, the cost won't be more than a few hundred dollars.

• **Step 2**—*Treif* Busters: If you like spring-cleaning, you will love this step. This is when you are going to dispose of every last trace of nonkosher food in your home—not to mention those old forks you've been wanting to get rid of anyway. You may be able to donate certain items to a local food bank or shelter. You know that stack of frozen shrimp dinners in your freezer? Well, it's time to say goodbye. Those six cans of bacon-flavored baked beans? Bye bye. And say so long to those extra crunchy Cajun cheese curls made with real cheddar. Double Stuffed Oreo cookies? Thank goodness, those you can keep.

• **Step 3**—Rub-a-Dub-Dub: It's now time to break out the Mr. Clean. At this point, you are going to give your kitchen the most thorough cleaning it's ever had. Every shelf and cabinet—clear it out, wash it down, and make way for kosher food! Do the same for the fridge. Tables, countertops, sinks—rub-a-dub-dub. When you're done, you will be staring at a kitchen that looks a lot like it did before the very first owner of the house ever moved in.

• **Step 4**—Flamethrowers: This is the heavy moving and lifting part—the part where you will be implementing the halachic procedures necessary to transform items such as your stovetop, oven, cutlery, microwave oven, and favorite can opener from treif to 100 % grade A kosher. At this point, you need to be especially careful because this is the one and only time you will be kashering your kitchen—this is going to impact you, your family, and your friends for years and even generations to come—and you want to be sure to get it right.

• **Step 4.5**—Ever Seen a Wok Swim? This step has little—and everything—to do with kosher food. This is where you will learn about immersing your cookware and other utensils in a special kind of Jewish pool known as a *mikvah*. This step has little to do with kosher food because if you skip it completely, your food will still be kosher. At the same time, it has everything to do with kosher because kosher eating is much more about the soul than it is about the body, and the *mikvah* has everything to do with spiritually elevating the whole realm of food and eating.

• **Step 5**—Kosher Importers Inc.: The final step is the easiest part and the most fun. This is where you restock your kitchen with nothing but kosher food. By the way, you will probably find that 50–80 percent of the products in your home, other than meat and cheese, are already kosher.

Now, let's get down to business.

STEP I—CRATE AND BARREL

At this point you will need to create three lists: one for items that don't need to be koshered at all and can continue to be friendly parts of your kitchen, one for items that need to be kashered before they can be used in your new kosher kitchen, and one for items that simply have to go.

List I—Kosher Just the Way They Are

As long as the following items were never used for cooking, with hot foods, or washed in your dishwasher, they only need to be thoroughly cleaned and do not require any further kashering process. Of course, if you have been looking for a good excuse to get rid of those old ice cube trays and want to celebrate this wonderful occasion of kashering your kitchen by splurging on some new kitchen items, that's perfectly fine. If you're not sure whether a specific item requires kashering, be sure to consult with the person who is coaching you through this process.

- Refrigerators
- Storage shelves and cabinets
- Tables and chairs
- Countertops
- High chairs
- Glass cups and mugs
- Crystal glasses
- Glass, Corelle, Pyrex, Arcoroc, and Duralex items that were not used for cooking directly on a heat source.
- Cup and banana trees (those things with hooks on which coffee cups, bananas, or other items are hung)
- Towel racks
- Cookie jars
- Breadbaskets
- Ice cube trays
- Storage bins and baskets; plastic, wicker, Tupperware, and other containers that are only used to store items such as beans, rice, pasta, and dry cereal
- Napkin holders
- Sugar bowls
- Spice racks
- Measuring cups and spoons (provided they were not used with hot liquids or foods)
- Can and bottle openers
- Corkscrews
- Wine racks
- Dish towels, pot holders, and oven mitts (will require laundering)
- Fruit bowls
- Candy and nut dishes
- Plastic salad bowls
- Ice buckets
- Vegetable peelers

List 2—Presto Chango

All of these items can be kashered. Some require more effort to be kashered, some require less effort, and some will depend on the kashering method your rabbi recommends. The specific methods for kashering are on page 157–163.

Myths&Facts

Myth: Kosher is actually an ancient Jewish health code. The reason pork is not kosher is because undercooked meat, particularly pork, often contains trichinae, which cause trichinosis. Modern methods of food production and preparation have all but eliminated most of the health concerns that were once prevalent in foods and have made kosher obsolete.

Fact: Kosher is about spirituality and holiness and is a central element in the grand scheme of Jewish living. Kosher foods may have incidental health benefits, but the reason Jews eat kosher is because the Torah requires it.

1. Ovens — Gas, electric, nuclear; they can all be kashered.

2. Stove top burners — No problem.

3. Microwave oven — May be a problem. Let your rabbi be your guide.

4. Kitchen sink

5. Bathtub   Difficult to kasher, but why would you want to?

6. Gas or charcoal grill   Now you're getting tricky.

7. Toaster oven

8. Broiler

9. Dishwasher   A bit of a problem, but not insurmountable.

10. Blender

11. Mixer   If you can clean it, you can kasher it.

12. Food processor

13. Metal pots   This includes steel, aluminum, iron, and kryptonite. Pot handles can present a problem. Metal handles that are either part of the pot or removable are no problem. Plastic handles that can be removed are also not a problem, but pots with plastic handles that can't be removed may not be kasherable.

14. Steel cutlery   As easy as boiling a pot of water.

15. Plastic colander   Bye-bye.

16. Plastic utensils   Yes? No? Maybe? You'd better seek advice.

List 3—This Stuff Has Got to Go—Probably

This list consists of two types of items. The first type includes items that just can't be kashered and that you will have to part with. The second type includes items that are either very difficult to kasher or that only a minority of opinions on Jewish law (halacha) allow to be kashered. With regard to this second type, it is advisable that you consult with your kashering coach or rabbi.

Here are a few generalizations:

• Most items made of metal or wood, as long as they have no nicks, chips, or scratches beneath the surface, can be kashered. (Plastic is more difficult.)

• Earthenware, such as china, pottery, porcelain, and ceramic, cannot be kashered.

• Sterling silver and silver-plated items can be kashered. These items, however, can be tricky to clean because they often have intricate decorative details on them. For this reason, they require special care when they are being kashered.

Now for the specifics:

1. Silverware: Cutlery that is made of two pieces of material and that has a gap between the two pieces cannot be kashered. The most common examples are knives where the blade is made of stainless steel and the handle is made of wood or plastic. If this sounds like your set of flatware, consult your coach: it may be time to donate it to Goodwill or a homeless shelter.

2. Toaster: If you have ever toasted nonkosher bread or other nonkosher foods, such as Pop-Tarts or toaster waffles, then it's time to get that new super-duper toaster you have had your eye on.

3. Frying pans: These pans have seen their last omelet.

4. George Foreman grill: It's a knockout. You will need to get a new one.

5. Teflon: Most likely, your Teflon-coated pots and pans are history. In some cases, however, they can be kashered.

6. Cake pans and muffin tins: Say bye-bye.

7. China: This is where kashering can be painful: china can't be kashered. In certain limited instances, as in the case of heirloom china, there may be a procedure for kashering that can be done after the items are not used for a year. Again consult your coach.

8. Corning Ware: It has got to go. You were probably hoping that Jewish law considers Corning Ware to be like glass (which can be kashered), but it is actually considered to be a type of earthenware.

9. Chopsticks: If they are wood, they're history.

10. Wooden mixing bowl: Wood can be kashered, but if the surface has any cracks or deep scratches, the process won't work. If the bowl was never used for hot foods, it only needs to be cleaned.

11. Wooden rolling pin: It's probably got scratches, so plan on getting a new one.

STEP 2—TREIF BUSTERS

This is a time of transition, and once you have completed step 2, there is no looking back. You are now going to dispose of all of the nonkosher food in your home, all of the kitchen items that cannot be kashered, and even some of the memories associated with those things. For example,

1. Your favorite box of chocolates: Yes, the box your husband got you for your anniversary. That's it. No more.

2. That jar of spicy salsa: Yes, the salsa you have every year at your Super Bowl party. Drop it directly into the garbage. (And while you are at it, you can also finally let go of the pain and agony associated with watching your team lose the big game, if it ever made it that far.)

3. Marshmallow-stuffed cookies: Anyone who has made the switch will tell you, even years later, that despite the fact that you can find virtually anything you want with a *hechsher*, some things just can't be replaced. Marshmallow goodies are one of them. Kosher marshmallow cookies and marshmallow ice cream are hard to find. However, there are plain old kosher marshmallows for roasting over a campfire, though they too can be tough to find. But that's the way it goes—we all make sacrifices.

4. Spoons: Yes, those three plastic-handled spoons from your college days that you still have in the drawer. It's time to let go.

5. Grandma's frying pan: Grandma used to make you eggs in that pan, and now you use it to make eggs for your kids. This is a tough one. You could frame it and hang it in the family room, but somehow it just won't be the same.

6. Your chopsticks: I know, you bought them in San Francisco's Chinatown on what was one of the greatest vacations of your life. You order in Chinese food almost every Sunday, those chopsticks are like an extension of your hand, and when you pick them up you can still see the chilly fog rolling in over the Golden Gate Bridge. (They're just chopsticks—toss them out already!)

This step in the process is actually a profound one. It represents the potential that we all have to change and to grow. It's about our ability to dislodge ourselves from patterns of living that are habitual but not necessarily beneficial. It's a step that reminds us that it's never too late to make genuine changes that will reverberate throughout our lives for years to come, put us in touch with deeper dimensions of our identity, and enable us to express deeper aspects of who we are and who we want to be. So embrace this moment. It's a big step—not necessarily an easy one but one that you can be proud of and that can always serve as a reminder that when the need arises, you are capable of bold changes and dramatic growth.

STEP 3—RUB-A-DUB-DUB

The big day is rapidly approaching, and soon you will be the proud owner of a beautiful new kosher kitchen. But first, it's time to roll up your sleeves.

The method for cleaning your kitchen that I am about to suggest is exceptionally thorough, but if you do follow it, you will feel great. (And if you hire a cleaning service to help, you may feel even better.)

Cleaning the Kitchen—the Whole Kitchen

You can go about cleaning the kitchen in one of two ways: the every-nook-and-cranny approach or the bare-necessities approach. As a rule, I recommend the every-nook-and cranny approach, but this is a personal issue that I leave up to you and your kashering coach to discuss.

THE EVERY-NOOK-AND-CRANNY APPROACH

The first approach requires some forethought because you are going to need a place to put a lot of stuff for the day. Here's what you do:

Empty your kitchen of everything—that's right, everything. Take all the food in every cabinet, all the pots and pans, everything on every countertop, and put it all in the room closest to the kitchen. The same goes for the refrigerator and freezer, though here some sanity is appropriate, so don't leave perishable items out for too long.

At this point, your kitchen will look like it did the day before you moved in, only dustier. What you are going to do now is simple: it's called cleaning. I mean every countertop, every drawer, every tabletop, the seats of all the chairs—everything. Using soap and water you will clean it, rinse it, and dry it. And then, put everything back, making sure nothing nonkosher sneaks in by mistake.

The Talmud is composed of thirty-six volumes that cover all of Jewish law, practice, and philosophy. The first volume is called Berachot (Blessings). The blessings that a person says before and after eating food are the way by which we recognize and acknowledge that all blessings come from God. This is where all of Judaism begins, with an appreciation that everything is from God and that everything we benefit from and enjoy in life is a blessing from our Creator.

THE BARE-NECESSITIES APPROACH

In the second approach, all you need to do is clean tabletops and countertops and proceed directly to the next step. It is advisable, even for bare-necessities people, to make sure that all refrigerator shelves and drawers are clean of any food residue from old sticky spills.

Cleaning the Items That Are to Be Kashered

Everything to be kashered—stove, silverware, sink, and anything else—requires two steps prior to kashering.

The first step is cleaning. The surface of all items must be completely clean of any food residue and even of any rust. The second step is the actual kashering process. To kasher a pot or anything else, you must expose the entire surface area to the kashering agent (fire or water). For metal surfaces, you will probably need a lot of steel wool and a lot of elbow grease. This step can be a lot of work, and it's absolutely necessary.

Here are some specifics:

• Pots and pot handles: If the pot handles can be removed, then they must be. The pot, the removable handle, and the surface area between the handle and the pot need to be cleaned.

• Silverware: Clean silverware thoroughly, making sure no particles of food remain. Serrated knives are notorious for trapping bits of food between their teeth. Food also likes to hide between the tines of forks, so keep your eyes open.

• Gas or electric oven: The oven is frequently the most difficult item to clean. Invariably, old spills are baked onto the walls or floor of the oven. And guess what? You have to get them off. Clean the oven thoroughly with an oven cleaner, and then use steel wool to scrub off anything that remains. Once the surface is clean, run the oven at 500 degrees, or the highest setting, for forty minutes. Once again, this is a time when you will want to consult closely with your coach.

• Self-cleaning oven: The intense heat produced by the self-cleaning feature cleans and kashers the oven simultaneously. A self-cleaning oven needs no prior cleaning.

• Gas and electric stovetops: Electric burners need to be removed and cleaned. Gas grates on which the pots sit need to be kashered. It is easy enough to purchase new drip pans, though they can also be removed and cleaned. The stovetop also needs to be thoroughly cleaned.

• Kitchen sink: The sink needs to be cleaned thoroughly, and if any raised bits of food residue don't come off, you should use steel wool.

• Microwave oven: Clean thoroughly. You will probably need a toothpick to get bits of food out of crevices where the walls meet one another.

• Food processor: The jar, lid, and blades all need to be cleaned well. The same is true for blenders, mixers, juicers, ice cream makers, and other small appliances.

Once you have finished cleaning everything, you will be ready to begin the final and most ambitious step in the kashering process. This is when you will actually kasher all your items and thereby transform them into vessels that are completely suitable for use in any kosher kitchen anywhere. But not so fast—as a rule, you will need to wait twenty-four hours from the time you have finished cleaning an item until you can actually kasher it. So after completing your big day of cleaning, I suggest you treat yourself to dinner at your favorite kosher restaurant and then get a good night's sleep before putting the final touches on your new kosher kitchen.

STEP 4—FLAMETHROWERS
This is the part where a knowledgeable coach really comes in handy. You want to make sure that you are doing things just right (even if you have read this book ahead of time), and it's easier and a lot more fun to do this with someone else.

Kashering 101: The Basics
The purpose of the kashering process is to transform utensils that had once been used with nonkosher foods and are therefore "personae non grata" in a kosher kitchen into utensils that are 100 percent permissible for kosher use. Contrary to urban legend, the process does not involve magic wands or voodoo. The kashering process is a logical, straightforward method of

purging any nonkosher residue from cookware and other utensils. Kashering not only comes into play when someone begins to keep kosher but also in any kosher home where an item may have been used inadvertently with nonkosher food. In such a case, the kashering process enables the owner to restore the item to its kosher status and to avoid the expense of replacement.

The objective of kashering is to rid utensils of surface residue as well as any traces of food that have been absorbed by the utensil. For surface residue, a thorough cleaning is usually sufficient. For absorbed residue, the utensil must be purged in the same fashion that it was initially used with nonkosher food. For example, a pot in which nonkosher soup was cooked needs to be kashered by boiling. A roasting pan used in a nonkosher oven will require a different method of kashering.

Kashering 101: The Three Steps

For a utensil to be kashered it needs to go through a three-step process:

1. The utensil must be thoroughly cleaned of any surface matter, food, rust, and other unidentifiable stuff.

2. The utensil may not be used for twenty-four hours prior to being kashered.

3. The utensil must be kashered in the same fashion that it was generally used for cooking in the past.

Kashering 101: Practically Speaking

The following is a list of the most common items that require kashering and a brief explanation of the method. Again, I don't recommend doing this on your own.

Important note: Please be aware that regarding some of the items below there are disputes in Jewish law regarding if and how an item can be kashered. The methods below are accepted by most rabbinic authorities in most communities; however, I suggest that you consult carefully with your rabbi or coach.

ITEMS THAT CAN BE BOILED

Many items can be kashered by boiling. To do this you will need a large, clean, kosher pot that hasn't been used for twenty-four hours. Fill the pot with water and bring the water to a rolling boil. Immerse each item to be kashered while the water is boiling. If the item is too large to be dropped in the pot and totally covered by the water, you can dip one part in and then dip the other part in. Keep in mind that immersing items may drop the temperature of the water below the boiling point. For this reason, it's advisable to wait a few seconds between immersions to make sure the water is boiling each time you drop something in. Remember, boiling water may kasher forks but it scalds fingers, so be careful. I advise wearing oven mitts and using tongs to remove items from the water. Use extra caution if children are helping. When items are removed from the water, they need to be briefly rinsed in cold or room temperature water.

The following items are all kashered by boiling:
1. Silverware and cutlery
2. Blender jar, blade, and lid
3. Blender blade
4. Spaetzle maker
5. Carving knives
6. Cheese grater
7. Olive stoner
8. Some plastic bowls
9. Poultry shears
10. Mixing bowls
11. Potato peeler
12. Serving utensils
13. Ice cream scooper
14. Metal pots
15. And many more

OVENS

Different types of ovens have different heating and engineering characteristics. These variations affect the manner in which ovens are kashered.

- Self-cleaning oven: A self-cleaning oven is a kashering dream come true. All you need to do is run the oven through the cleaning cycle and it's kosher. The reason for this is that the oven gets so hot that it burns off everything.
  You can also use your self-cleaning oven to kasher other metal items. Your rabbi or coach will explain.

- Conventional oven: Once you have completed your thorough cleaning, run the oven on broil for forty minutes.

- Convection oven: Extra care needs to be taken when cleaning a convection oven. Don't forget to clean the fan and chute. Once the oven is clean, forty minutes on the highest setting will do the trick.

- Continuous cleaning: Run the oven on broil for forty minutes. If it's totally clean after that, then you are good to go.

STOVETOPS

- Electric: Turn the burners to high and once they have become red-hot for a few minutes, they are kosher.

- Gas: You have two options here:
  1. Place the metal grates in your oven while it is being kashered. Both the oven and the grates will be simultaneously kashered.
  2. Spread a double layer of heavy duty aluminum foil over the grates, turn the flames to high, and after ten minutes the grates will be kosher.

SINKS

Some materials can be easily kashered, some are more difficult, and some can't be kashered at all. The type of material a sink is made of will determine if and how it can be kashered.

- Stainless steel: Boiling water from a kosher kettle needs to be poured over every square inch of the sink, including the spout and the drain. It usually takes a few kettles of water to make sure that a boiling stream hits every spot of the surface area. After kashering your sink, you will need separate racks, mats, or basins for when you wash or use meat dishes and dairy dishes in the sink.

- Porcelain: Porcelain and china sinks can't be kashered, so you will need to buy a whole new house. Or, if your budget can't handle that, you will need to wash the sink thoroughly, not use it for twenty-four hours, and then use separate racks, mats, or basins for milk dishes and meat dishes when you use the sink.

- Corian: You'd better speak with your rabbi about this one.

I'd Better Ask

- Granite: Granite sinks are kashered in the same fashion as stainless steel sinks. For sinks made of a granite composite, check with your rabbi.

Important notice: In addition to having separate racks for milk dishes and meat dishes, you will also need separate sponges, sponge dishes, and scouring pads for milk, meat, and pareve use.

MICROWAVE OVEN

The glass plate at the bottom of the oven is kashered by pouring boiling water over the entire surface area. As for the oven itself, there is more than one method of kashering, so whatever your rabbi suggests will be the method for you.

DISHWASHER

Stainless steel dishwashers can be kashered. All other dishwashers are much more problematic and require rabbinic guidance.

The dishwasher consists of two parts: the racks and the dishwasher itself.

• The racks: Ideally, you should purchase new racks. If you can't, the racks should be thoroughly cleaned and not used for twenty-four hours, after which boiling water is poured on them.

• The dishwasher: Everything needs to be cleaned thoroughly: the walls, traps, strainers, drains, and revolving spray arms. Once the cleaning is finished, don't use the dishwasher for twenty-four hours. To kasher the dishwasher, you will need to run it through three extra-hot cycles. You get extra-hot water by turning your water heater to its highest setting two hours before running the first wash cycle. Caution: The hot water in all your sinks will now be dangerously hot, so make sure everyone in the house, especially children, is very careful. And don't forget to turn down the temperature when you have finished the third cycle.

Keep in mind that your dishwasher can be used only for milk or meat dishes, so you will have to make a choice, and once you do, there is no turning back. You can, of course, invest in a second dishwasher and use one for milk and one for meat.

TOASTER OVEN AND BROILER

The toaster oven and broiler are kashered in the same fashion as a conventional oven.

BARBECUE GRILL

Grills are tough to kasher but not impossible. The goal is to get the grates and any part of the inside of the grill that has come in direct contact with food red-hot. For a gas grill, cover the grates with a metal cover of heavy duty foil, and then turn the gas to high. For charcoal, pile a mountain of briquettes up to the grate, cover the grate with another couple of layers of briquettes, light your fire, and stand back.

STEP 4.5—EVER SEEN A WOK SWIM?

Kosher food is one thing, but kosher salad bowls—what's that all about? Not only does our food need to be kosher, but even our muffin tins, ladles, and Crock-Pot slow cookers need to be kosher, so to speak. As we have discussed, food and eating are brimming with latent spirituality. The food we eat, the blessings we say, our attitudes toward nourishing the body, our view of the very tables we dine at, and even the pots and pans we cook in—everything surrounding our interaction with food is invested with great potential for meaning and sanctity.

When we say that our utensils need to be kosher, we mean that they need to go through a kind of spiritual metamorphosis. This process is called *tevilah*, or dipping, and is accomplished by dipping utensils in a special body of water known as a *mikvah*. A *mikvah* is a natural body of water such as a lake or an ocean, or a specially designed pool of water that is fed by rainwater. *Mikvah* waters, like the waters that surround an unborn child, are the waters through which a profound transition and transformation takes place.

The Role of the Mikvah

When the Temple stood in Jerusalem, the *mikvah* played a central role in the spiritual life of the Jewish people. Immersion in *mikvah* waters is also the final step on the transformational path that a non-Jew takes when converting to Judaism. The *mikvah* also has a special role in elevating a Jewish marriage as well as in contributing to the elevated status of our relationship to food.

Many of the new utensils you will purchase, as well as those you will be keeping, need to be dipped in a *mikvah* in order to become full-fledged members of your new kosher kitchen. Preparing food in cookware that has not been dipped in a *mikvah*, or using plates and cutlery that haven't swum in a *mikvah*, does not technically make your food nonkosher. But what is gained through the *mikvah* is an elevated spiritual dimension to food that is distinct from, yet deeply related to, kashrut.

Following are lists of items that require immersion in a *mikvah* and those that don't. Once again, you will want to consult with your rabbi or coach about the specific application of these rules.

All items that come into direct contact with food either during food preparation or when food is eaten need to be immersed if they are made of any one of the following materials:

- Steel
- Aluminum
- Copper
- Iron
- Silver
- Gold
- Lead
- Tin
- Brass
- Glass
- Pyrex
- Duralex
- Corelle
- China
- Corning Ware
- Stoneware
- Porcelain

The following items do not require a trip to the *mikvah*:

- Containers used only for food storage (and not at the table), such as cookie jars or pasta containers.

• Single-use aluminum products, such as disposable pans and baking sheets.

• All refrigerator or pantry shelves, regardless of what they are made of.

Items used for eating or food preparation do not require immersion if they are made of the following materials:

• Wood
• Stone
• Paper
• Plastic
• Styrofoam
• Unglazed earthenware

To Bless or Not to Bless: That is the Question

We have already seen that there are special blessings one says prior to eating. A special blessing is also made before immersing many, though not all, utensils in a *mikvah*. I suggest you discuss the technicalities of which items do or don't require a blessing with your coach. The blessing to be said is as follows:

Blessed are You God our Lord, Sovereign of the universe, Who has sanctified us with His commandments and commanded us to immerse utensils.

בָּרוּךְ אַתָּה יהוה אֱלֹהֵינוּ מֶלֶךְ הָעוֹלָם אֲשֶׁר קִדְּשָׁנוּ בְּמִצְוֹתָיו וְצִוָּנוּ עַל טְבִילַת כֵּלִים

Baruch atah Adonai, Elohaynu melech ha-olam, asher k'dshanu b'mitzvotav, v'tzivanu al t'vilat kaylim.

Soul Food

• •

The book of Va'yikra (the third of the Five Books of the Torah), contains an extensive section that devotes forty-seven verses to the laws of kosher and nonkosher foods, including meat, poultry, fish, and insects. The following are the three concluding verses:

I am God who elevates you from the land Egypt in order to be your God; and you should be holy because I am holy. This is the instruction regarding the animal, the bird, and every living being that lives in the water, and every creature that crawls on the ground. There is a distinction between those that are impure and those that are pure, between the creature that may be eaten, and the one that may not be eaten.

Lev. 11: 45–47

The classical commentaries on the Torah derive the following idea from these verses:

The Jewish nation wasn't just taken *out* from Egypt, they were *elevated* from Egypt. The whole purpose of the Exodus from Egypt was so that the Jewish people could receive the Torah and thereby be able to lead an elevated, spiritual existence. The laws of kosher food are so profoundly central to a Jew living an elevated, godly, spiritual life that if the only rules the Torah contained were the ones about kosher food, they alone would have justified the entire Exodus and birth of the Jewish nation.

• •

STEP 5—KOSHER IMPORTERS INC.

The hard part is over and now the fun begins. You can fill your kitchen with nothing but kosher food and cook your first homemade kosher feast.

You will find that shopping for kosher food is far easier than most people imagine. That's because these days a huge percentage of foods at your local grocery are kosher.

Ice cream? No problem. Ben and Jerry's, Godiva, Häagen-Dazs, and others are kosher. Indian curry veggie burgers? No problem. You can choose from Bombay, California, charbroiled, and "chicken" nugget veggie dishes in the freezer section. And if you are one of those low-carb, high-protein energy-bar people, you will be pleasantly surprised when you visit that section in the health food store. Breakfast cereals? The majority are kosher. Crab cakes? Yes, you can even get mock crabmeat. Cheetos? Though they're not kosher yet, there are kosher brands of cheese curls and similar snack foods. You can't live without Trader Joe's sprouted wheat sesame seed bagels? Don't worry , you won't have to. You like unusual sodas like Jones Green Apple, Blue Bubblegum, and Fufu Berry sodas? (I'm not making this up.) They are all kosher, and so is Jones Turkey and Gravy flavored soda. If you love cooking with olive oil the way I do, you're in luck. From Wal-Mart's brand to Lucini Italia and even Les Huileries de Menkes from Morocco, all are kosher. Cookies? How about Famous Amos, Oreo, Newman's Own, Pepperidge Farm, and Fig Newton for starters? Plain old pasta? It's practically impossible to find one that *isn't* kosher. Are you a snack food person? I hope you will be able to survive on Bugles, Pringles, Heinz ketchup chips, and Blue Terra chips.

You get the picture. Now go ahead, eat in your new home—and enjoy.

MAZEL TOV!

You did it. You kashered your home and more firmly planted your personal spiritual roots in the rich soil of Jewish life, Jewish history, and the destiny of the Jewish people. By this point you will be a bit exhausted, yet at the same time you will realize that you have achieved a great milestone in your life. Maybe it's not as big as marriage or your first child, but becoming another link in a spiritual chain that connects countless Jewish homes around the globe and across the ages is nothing to sneeze at. And even if you haven't yet kashered your home, remember that Judaism isn't all or nothing, and whatever you are doing to expand your Jewish horizons is wonderful.

IT'S THE LAW!

KOSHER COP

Beware the parmesan

While we must wait after eating meat before eating dairy, there is no parallel requirement after first eating dairy. It is therefore permissible to have a cup of coffee and a cheese Danish as a snack and then proceed directly to a dinner of barbecued chicken. The only requirement is to wash one's hands, rinse one's mouth and have a bit of something pareve after consuming dairy. There is one exception: in the case of certain hard cheeses, one must wait six hours until eating meat. A hard cheese is defined as one that has been aged for six months. The vast majority of kosher cheeses are not "hard," though beware the parmesan because some parmesans are indeed hard cheese.

Chapter 6
Ten Questions People Ask about Kosher

QUESTION 1:

What is the difference between kosher food, a kosher kitchen, and a kosher home?

ANSWER:

Kosher food is any food whose consumption is not prohibited by Jewish law and is prepared and manufactured in accordance with Jewish law.

"Kosher kitchen" is a term used to describe the kitchen in a home where the laws of kosher are carefully adhered to. For instance, a kosher kitchen is one that has two separate sets of plates, cutlery, and cookware—one for dairy foods and the other for meat. A kosher kitchen will often have two separate ovens—one for meat and one for dairy. Some kosher kitchens will also feature separate meat and dairy sinks, though most people consider this to be a luxury. Having two separate dishwashers is also in the luxury category, separate refrigerators are almost unheard of, and two totally separate kitchens are only for people who have won the lottery.

"Kosher home" is a colloquial term that refers to a household where the laws of kosher are carefully observed. It's not unusual for Jews who are discussing their upbringing to say that they were or were not raised in a "kosher home." This is an unofficial way for people to indicate the degree to which Judaism was or wasn't practiced in their home, though it is not necessarily a genuine litmus test for one's overall relationship to Judaism.

INSIGHT:

To be born and raised in a free country, a country defined and characterized by freedom, by the recognition of so many basic yet profound human rights, and by great opportunity, is a blessing and a privilege. Yet it is easy to take all of these blessings for granted and to forget just how fortunate we Americans are.

To be a Jew, to be a part of a remarkably unique people that has given so much to mankind, is also a profound blessing and a privilege of the highest order. If the observance of kosher served no other purpose than the regular, daily reminder that one is a Jew—an honored member of an esteemed group of people—then this alone would be of great importance. People can forget about almost anything in life, but they can't forget to eat, and every time Jews eat they remember what is perhaps the most important thing that any person needs to know: who they are.

QUESTION 2:

Who says Jews have to keep kosher?

ANSWER:

The Torah says so. The Torah (Jewish Bible), in the book of Leviticus, chapter 11, delineates the major categories of kosher and nonkosher foods. There, the Torah specifies the species of animals, fish, and birds that are considered kosher; those that are not; and the concept of not eating dairy and meat together.

The Torah also explicitly outlaws the eating of blood and of meat torn from a live animal or from an animal that wasn't properly slaughtered. In addition to the general rules of kosher food laid down by the Torah, the Talmud (Oral Tradition) goes into detail about the specific application of the laws in the Torah. Two of the most well-known areas of kosher law that are detailed in the Talmud are the rules related to the kosher slaughtering of animals and preparation of meats and the specifics of not eating or even cooking meat and milk products together.

INSIGHT:

The aspect of kashrut that has the most far-reaching effect on people who keep kosher is the rule about the separation of milk and meat. This not only means that cheeseburgers are a no-no, but it also means that in their kitchens, people must maintain separate sets of cookware, dishes, and utensils for milk and meat; that almost all kosher restaurants come in two styles, meat or dairy; and that after enjoying a good steak for dinner, you can't have ice cream for dessert—not even an hour later!

This is the perfect spot for a very important aside; an aside about the Talmud. You see, while the Talmud is not only central to the laws of kosher, but also to much of Jewish life, it is also frequently misunderstood. So here goes. Think of the next page as The Talmud in a Nutshell.

THE TALMUD IN A NUTSHELL

Avery important though little-known fact about the Torah is that the Torah actually has two parts. One part is world-famous, has been a bestseller in almost every language, and has been read and studied by people of every faith and background. The other part is far less well-known, almost defies translation, and has been studied by almost no one other than Jews for thousands of years. Part one (the really famous part) consists of the text of the Torah, is commonly called the Five Books of Moses, and is known to the world as the Bible. This is the text that is written on every Torah scroll in every synagogue. In classical Judaism, this text of the Five Books of Moses is known as the *Written Torah*. Part two (the less-famous part) is known as the *Oral Torah*, or Talmud. Classical Jewish tradition maintains that when the Jewish people received the Torah at Mount Sinai, they not only got two tablets but also got a Torah in two distinct parts, one written and one oral. The Oral Torah was, well, not written down. Its contents were studied, memorized, and carefully taught without the benefit of a source text; hence its name: the Oral Torah.

So now you probably want to know just what this Oral Torah consists of?

The oral part of the Torah is the detailed explanation of the text in the Written Torah. You see, taken on its own, the Written Torah is pretty tough to understand and can even be downright misleading if you don't have the accompanying explanation contained within the Oral Torah. Without the existence of the Oral Torah, the Written Torah is hopelessly incomplete. You just can't point to a Torah scroll in synagogue and say "that's the entire Torah," because it isn't. There is a whole other part of that Torah, the Oral Torah, that completes the unit and makes them one unified whole.

Here are two examples of how this symbiotic relationship between the Written Torah and Oral Torah works; one is about a holiday and the other is about kosher.

1. Sukkot is a wonderful holiday that takes place about a week after Yom Kippur. During Sukkot, families build a temporary dwelling where they eat their meals during the holiday. The Written Torah says, "In *sukkot* you shall live for seven days." The problem here is that it doesn't tell us what these *sukkot* are. Are they tents, tepees, igloos, or something altogether different from these other dwellings? If we had nothing at our disposal other than the Written Torah, then on the holiday of Sukkot, Jews would have built log cabins, lean-tos, and probably even customized *sukkot*-condos. But they didn't. As it turns out, the Oral Torah spells out quite precisely what a *sukkah* is. Thanks to the Oral Torah, wherever Jews have lived, their *sukkot* have always been constructed according to the same rules.

So there you have it: one Torah, two inseparable parts. Now that you are a bona fide Talmudic scholar, you will appreciate the Talmud at work as it relates to veal parmesan.

2. The written Torah says, "You shall not cook a baby goat in its mother's milk." In fact, the Written Torah repeats this statement three times. A reader who had no access to the Talmud could easily draw the conclusion that God finds cooking young goat meat in maternal milk to be particularly offensive; why else harp on the same issue three times? This is where the Oral Torah steps in.

The Talmud teaches that each one of these three statements is actually an allusion to a different aspect of the laws governing the separation of milk and meat. The first statement means that milk and meat cannot be *consumed* together, the second that they can't be *cooked*

together—even if one is not going to partake of the dish—
and the third that one can't realize any *profit* or personal
benefit from a mixture of milk and meat.

Whether in the kitchen, in the courtroom, or during the
celebration of any holiday, the key to implementing what the
Torah requires is to understand that when we say "Torah," we
mean the Written Torah and the Oral Torah together.

QUESTION 3:

What's the story with kosher symbols on packaged foods?

ANSWER:

When it comes to kosher food, "almost" isn't good
enough. A food product made with nine out of ten
kosher ingredients, is still 100 percent nonkosher. For
this reason, and because the food industry employs
highly sophisticated processes for making the
mountains of foods we eat, it is necessary to have someone who
is an expert both in the laws of kosher and in the intricacies of
food production to oversee the manufacture of kosher foods.

The person who fills this role is known as a *mashgiach*, or
supervisor. In most cases, the *mashgiach* is not an independent
contractor but works for one of the large national kosher certification organizations. Each of these organizations has a
trademarked symbol that lets the kosher consumer know that
the food production process has been supervised and okayed by
a qualified *mashgiach*.

INSIGHT:

Across the United States and around the world, thousands of
people have the job of ensuring the kashrut (kosherness) of

hundreds of thousands of food products consumed by millions of Jews to whom kosher food is of the utmost importance. The kosher food supervision business—no matter how sophisticated it becomes—will always be based on a few simple, intangible concepts: devotion, integrity, and trust. The entire kosher food industry, from the smallest deli to the brewery that makes Samuel Adams beers, rests on the shoulders of people who are devoted to Judaism and the teachings of the Torah. These people, above all else, are governed in their actions by a belief system that dates back over three thousand years. Those who oversee kashrut believe that God gave the Torah to the Jewish people and that the commandments related to kosher food are every bit as important, holy, and timeless as "Thou shall not steal" or the command to hear the sound of a shofar on Rosh Hashanah. Similarly, the millions of people who rely on the kosher food supervisors do so with complete trust. They trust that just as they don't relate to kosher food as a quaint ethnic ritual but as a vital part of a Jew's spiritual life, those they rely on view kosher with the same sense of gravity.

QUESTION 4:

Can pork chops ever be kosher?

ANSWER:

A pig is a pig, and no matter how you slice one, it can't ever be kosher. However, there does seem to be a ray of hope for kosher consumers who can't sleep at night because they wonder what pork chops taste like. It's called "tofu," and—who knows?—just as you can find tofurkey (tofu turkey) at your neighborhood natural grocery before Thanksgiving and tofu dogs to barbecue on the Fourth of July, someday there might just

be a tofork chop. (And when there is, you will even be able to have ice cream for dessert.)

INSIGHT:

The Talmud itself addresses the issue of Divine compensation for the fact that Jews will never ever be able to taste a succulent piece of ham: Consider the following:

For all foods forbidden by the Torah, there is a permissible food with a similar taste.

Talmud, Chulin 109b

The question, of course, is, Why is it important for a kosher taste equivalent to exist for pork, escargot, cicadas, or any other nonkosher food? The answer touches on a little-known Jewish concept about the very purpose of human existence.

At one time or another, almost every person asks the question, What's it all about? At issue is what is *life* all about. The Jewish understanding is that life is about achieving the pleasures of living. Of course, life has all sorts of pleasures. Swimming is a pleasure, having children is a pleasure, helping someone in need is a pleasure, cotton candy is a pleasure, love is a pleasure, fighting for a just cause is a pleasure, and so forth. All of these are pleasures—some more meaningful and sublime than others but all pleasures nonetheless.

When you think about the array of physical pleasures available to us, you could possibly conclude that God went a little overboard. After all, the world has over 250,000 flowering plants, each with its own unique shape, coloring, and scent. Wouldn't orchids, roses, irises, and maybe a few dozen other flowers have sufficed? Consider the following:

The blue of the sky, the green of the trees, the beautiful hues of the various flowers, the glory of the sunrise and sunset are but part of the happiness bestowed on man. The pleasure of smell is a remarkable happiness: the savor of foods, of baking, of spices . . . the pleasures of sound are also noteworthy and man has found happiness in music from the most ancient times. Perhaps many of these pleasures are not intended for man's happiness but merely to induce him to do what is necessary for his existence. [For this] The Creator could have forced man to eat by the mere desire to relieve the pain of hunger. The pleasure of eating and procreating is a gift from the Creator, and the purpose is to bestow kindliness on man.

Rabbi Avigdor Miller, *Rejoice O'Youth*

Myths & Facts

Myth: Kosher wines are thick, sweet, and unsophisticated.

Fact: Kosher wine is no longer limited to your grandfather's Concord Passover Seder wine. Today, if your palate favors a good Beaujolais, Pinot Grigio, Chardonnay, Merlot, Chenin Blanc, Cabernet Sauvignon, Gewurztraminer, Bordeaux, or Zinfandel, you'll find a large variety of high-quality kosher wines. Excellent kosher wines are now produced in France, Italy, Austria, Bulgaria, South Africa, Australia, and of course, Israel. California's Napa Valley is also home to some wonderful kosher wines that have won numerous gold and silver medals in many prestigious events. In 2003, the prestigious publication *Wine Spectator* gave twenty-three kosher wines ratings of eighty or higher, and the *Wall Street Journal* does an annual column on kosher wine.

Our sages tell us that when a person reaches heaven, one of the questions that person will be asked is, Why did you not enjoy the pleasures of life that you had the opportunity to enjoy?

In other words, if you have the chance to taste a bit of coriander and don't, God will one day look at you and say, "Whom do you think I created that stuff for anyway, Myself?"

Clearly, the Jewish understanding of life is that while Coke isn't really "it"—for there is far more to life than just physical pleasures—the endless array of physical pleasures were certainly created for us to enjoy, which brings us back to "tofork chops." It seems that God didn't want to deny the Jewish people any of the delectable tastes He created. So if Alaskan pollock can be made to taste like shrimp, then who knows? Tofu may be God's way of making sure we don't miss out on the taste of pork.

QUESTION 5:

Is it okay to eat kosher food in a nonkosher home or restaurant?

ANSWER:

Two issues come into play here. The first is the purely technical question about whether or not food from a nonkosher home or restaurant can ever actually be kosher. The second is an issue of perception.

1. Technical: The question of kosher food served or prepared in a nonkosher environment has many permutations; some are easy to address, and others can be quite difficult. Here are a few examples:

   • Kosher packaged goods (cookies, snack foods, nuts, etc.): To eat kosher foods directly from their original packaging—even in the middle of a Wendy's restaurant—completely avoids the problem of eating nonkosher food. Even if such foods were served on a plate, as long as the plate is clean and only kosher foods are on the plate, one can comfortably eat the food.

• Cooked kosher foods: Kosher food that is cooked together in the same oven as nonkosher food, and even kosher food cooked alone in an oven that has also been used for cooking nonkosher food, is rendered nonkosher through the cooking process. The issue is not one of guilt by association but rather is rooted in the intricate laws governing kosher food and the proper preparation of kosher food.

• Fresh fruit: Fresh, uncut fruits do not present any problems. They can be eaten at your local farmers' market, at the home of a non-Jewish friend, when purchased on the run in an airport, or anywhere else.

2. Perception: The question of perception has nothing to do with whether or not the food is actually kosher but rather with the concern that the projection of a false or confusing impression may inadvertently lead to someone else eating nonkosher food. The following examples illustrate:

• A Pepsi at Burger King: Let's say a man wearing a *kippa* (religious headgear) or a woman who everyone knows keeps kosher walks into a Burger King restaurant during his or her lunch break to buy a Pepsi. Now let's suppose that another Jewish person, one who doesn't fully keep kosher but is conscious of avoiding nonkosher food where possible, sees that person enter the Burger King. The second person could draw the following conclusion: "Gee, I know that person couldn't be going in there to get a hamburger for lunch, so it must be that the fish sandwich is okay to eat. That's good to know." The result of this is that the second person could go through the next seventy-five years of life enjoying Burger King fish sandwiches while at the same time thinking he or she is being careful about keeping kosher. This possibility, though somewhat remote, should be enough to persuade conspicuously kosher consumers to avoid Burger King, even if it's just for a Pepsi.

Zoro the fish

Young swordfish have a type of scale whose removal destroys the skin. Adult swordfish have no scales at all. Kosher fish must have scales that can be removed while leaving the skin intact. Bottom line: swordfish is not kosher.

• Hot dogs at a baseball stadium: At Camden Yards alone, where the Baltimore Orioles play baseball, over 400,000 hot dogs were consumed during the 2004 season. Now guess how many of those were kosher: about 18,000, or almost 5 percent. Those 18,000 hot dogs, though purchased and consumed in an environment flooded with nonkosher hot dogs, did not present a false impression problem because they were purchased at a special stand that only sells 100 percent kosher food.

• Coffee at Starbucks: I will leave the issue of whether or not *any* cup of coffee is worth four dollars for others to discuss. Our question, with regard to coffee shops such as Starbucks, is whether or not you can buy a kosher cup of coffee in an establishment that also sells items like pastries and salads. In this case, since virtually everyone who goes into a Starbucks is going for the coffee, and since the entire business is built around the discerning coffee drinker, there is no need to worry that someone who keeps kosher may send the false impression that the double decadent nut brownies might also be kosher.

INSIGHT:

One of the fringe benefits of keeping kosher is that it keeps you on your toes. Judaism encourages conscious living, the kind of living where people don't just pass through the day in a blur but where, as much as possible, one is present in every moment and every situation. Judaism asserts that to the extent we "space out," we miss out—on life. And one thing kosher does is foster aware, alert, conscious living.

QUESTION 6:

What is the difference between regular kosher and kosher for Passover?

ANSWER:

About three dollars a pound!

INSIGHT:

The truth is, "kosher for Passover" foods tend to be particularly expensive, and not without good reason. As you will see in chapter 7, the production of kosher food is far from simple. Topnotch kosher supervision requires not only expertise in a wide area of Jewish law but a sophisticated and up-to-the-minute knowledge of the intricacies of every aspect of the food production industry. This includes knowledge about stabilizers, alginates, natural flavors, BHA, and yellow number 4 (that one always makes me nervous), to name just a few, as well as knowledge about virtually every aspect of production from the farm until the lid is vacuum sealed on the jar. When it comes to Passover, in a sense this is doubly true. The reason for this is that a unique aspect of kosher is operative only during Passover and itself has numerous unique issues. This annual kosher phenomenon is called avoiding *chametz*.

Chametz is the term for all types of grain products that one is not permitted to eat on Passover. Foods that may be kosher throughout the year, are not necessarily "kosher for Passover." This is because products such as mayonnaise, iced tea, pickles, butter, yogurt, and Root Beer may contain small amounts of ingredients derived from grain and are therefore off-limits for Passover. Thus, the "kosher for Passover" labeling means that a particular product has been produced in accordance not only with the general rules of kosher food production but with the unique rules that apply to foods on Passover. So, even though our Passover grocery bills may seem a bit exorbitant, we must appreciate that behind every reputable "kosher for Passover" label stands an army of highly skilled experts. And it's thanks to them that we never have to go without barbecue-flavored potato chips—not during the year, and not even on Passover.

QUESTION 7:

Doesn't God have more important things to worry about than what I eat for breakfast?

ANSWER:

Yes, and no.

First, the yes: In the grand scheme of all existence—in the vastness of all God has created and in the grand unfolding drama of human history—there probably are a few things more important than what you or I had for breakfast this morning. Yet at the  same time, the answer is no. You see, from God's perspective, *everything* is of immense importance. This means that even if a scale of relative importance is used, the baseline starting point is considerably more significant than we realize.*

INSIGHT:

We all realize that attention to detail is critical and that the more serious the consequences of an action may be, the more important the details become. If you mistakenly dial a wrong phone number, the worst that will happen is getting an extra charge on your phone bill. If you hit "send" when you wanted to hit "delete" for an e-mail, *that* can be a big problem. If a recipe calls for two teaspoons of salt and instead you use two *tablespoons*, it's not the end of the world (unless, of course, you are baking for a state dinner at the White House). At the same time, one overlooked or misunderstood detail can lead to a medication with devastating unforeseen side effects being marketed to millions of consumers or can trigger a series of events that dooms a space shuttle and its crew.

We all take actions in the physical world seriously because we know we are dealing with real consequences. A deep, thoughtful Jewish life is one that takes the metaphysical as seriously as it does the physical. Jewish life is built on the recognition that attention to detail on the spiritual, metaphysical plane is no less important than it is on the physical. Our choice of breakfast cereals has both a nutritional impact on our bodies

*For a full treatment of this topic, see *Judaism In A Nutshell: God* by Shimon Apisdorf, Baltimore: Leviathan Press, 2001, 21–26.

and a spiritual impact on our souls, and to God, both are deeply important.

QUESTION 8:

Isn't the kosher method of slaughtering inhumane?

ANSWER:

Not at all. *Shechita* is by far the most humane form of animal slaughtering known to man, and to animals. *Shechita* is undoubtedly a very gory and bloody procedure, but that is part of what makes it so humane. Consider the following: Imagine going to a movie that garnered a PG13 rating because of "intense, disturbing images of torture and death." Now picture two scenes: in scene one, a master Samurai warrior cuts off the head of a prisoner with one blindingly rapid stroke of a ridiculously sharp sword. (While you keep on munching your popcorn.) In scene two, the master's young apprentice slowly twists the head of another prisoner round and round until he's finally dead. Which prisoner was afforded a more humane demise?

That's the difference between *shechita* and conventional methods of slaughtering. *Shechita* works like this: First, Jewish law requires that the special knife used for *shechita* must be literally sharper than a surgeon's blade. (A surgeon who would accidently cut himself with a surgical knife may not even realize it until he saw the blood.) Second, the *shochet* is a highly trained professional who must carefully check the sharpness of the blade after each cut. The slightest nick in the blade renders it invalid. Third, the swift *shechita* simultaneously severs the trachea, esophagus, and the two vagal nerves as well as the carotid arteries and jugular veins that are responsible for supplying blood to, and draining it from, the brain.

I have seen more than 100 cattle and a large number of sheep and calves slaughtered by the Jewish method of slaughtering. These observations were made in several slaughterhouses. The cutting of the throat is done so quickly and skillfully that the feeling of pain as a result of the cut is improbable. The contractions of the muscles of the animals, including struggling and sometimes convulsive movements following the cut, have nothing to do with consciousness or pain. An uninformed person watching the reactions of an animal dying from severe hemorrhage could draw erroneous conclusions with respect to consciousness and pain. Many physiologists and veterinarians in past years have declared in their opinion Shechita slaughter is humane and I join in this assertion.[6]

H.K. Dukes
Professor of Veterinary Physiology and Head of Department,
New York State Veterinary, Cornell University

Now consider the conventional method of slaughter. A special gun with a retractable, captive bolt is used to drive the bolt into the "sweet spot" of the animal's brain. This causes significant internal bleeding and the animal remains conscious longer than with *shechita*. When the bolt misses the sweet spot, which isn't uncommon, the animal is thrown into violently painful death spasms. It can take up to six shots to finally kill a big animal. And, even in such cases, the meat is still USDA approved for your grocer's deli! Not too many decades ago, when Jews were using the ancient, humane method of *shechita*, slaughterhouse workers were swinging sledge hammers at the heads of animals. And God only knows what their batting average was.

INSIGHT:

Judaism has two guiding principles that define the Jewish relationship to the animal kingdom. First, animals were created to serve the needs of mankind. Second, one is not permitted to cause an animal unnecessary, excessive, or gratuitous pain. Judaism places the value of human life, and the health and well-being of people, on a qualitatively higher plane than animal life. Bottom line: according to Judaism, not only are people *allowed* to benefit from animals, but we *should* benefit from them. If a load is too heavy for a person to carry, then rather than risking injury or wasting valuable time carrying a number of smaller loads, one should find the nearest donkey and load him up. At the same time, it is forbidden to overload the donkey, and if one sees an animal suffering under a heavy load, one must attempt to relieve the animal's burden. The same is true with benefiting from animal hides. If Eskimos need fur coats to survive, men need leather belts to keep their trousers up, and skiers need light weight down jackets to better navigate the moguls, that's just fine. However, if a kid wants to throw rocks at the local stray cat just "for the fun of it," no way; that is forbidden according to Jewish law. And there are scholarly Jewish opinions that say one is not even allowed to hurt a fly if it's not for the benefit of a person.

Myths & Facts

Myth: Americans pay a hidden kosher food tax because the FDA isn't good enough for Jews. By extorting large sums of money from food companies, Jews force up the price of food on thousands of products for millions of innocent Gentile consumers. The fees paid by companies to hundreds of orthodox rabbis go to line their pockets and fund other un-American activities.

Fact: This is an anti-Semitic canard that is promulgated by numerous racist groups that try to sow the seeds of hatred toward Jews in the minds of an unsuspecting public. The fact is that food companies of all kinds actively pursue kosher certification to increase their market share and boost their profit margin. The April 2005 issue of *Asia Food Journal*, a trade magazine for Asian food companies, ran a prominent article on kosher food that noted, among other things, "You may have Halal certification for the local [Muslim] markets. . . But if you want to sell your products further afield to other religious and health-minded consumers, you might need kosher certification too. Increasingly, big supermarket chains require kosher certification for own-label products. And more and more East Asian suppliers are finding that foreign companies need to know if their products are certified kosher." The cost of kosher certification is so nominal when compared to other production expenses that it has virtually no bearing on the price paid by the consumer.

QUESTION 9:

Some people eat kosher food at home but will eat nonkosher food in a restaurant or when they are at someone else's home. Isn't that hypocritical?

ANSWER:

No. A hypocrite is someone who espouses and claims to live by one standard but in fact lives by another. People who acknowledge a high ideal, only partially live up to it, and acknowledge that they are struggling to do their best are not hypocrites, just honest human beings.

INSIGHT:

Many myths exist about Judaism generally and about kosher in particular. One of the myths that relates to both is that Judaism is an all-or-nothing way of life. Nothing could be further from the truth—not in terms of Judaism as a whole and not in terms of kosher.

Judaism's paradigm for religiosity is a continuum, or process. Consider the following image from the life of Jacob, grandson of Abraham and Sarah and one of the founding fathers of the Jewish people:

> So Jacob left Beersheba and headed to Charan. He arrived at a certain place and spent the night there, and he dreamt. And in the dream was a ladder that stood firmly on the earth, while its top reached to the heavens. And the angels of God ascended and descended. And God was standing over him, and He said, 'I am the God of your father Abraham' . . .

> Gen. 28:10–13

Judaism views the spiritual life as a ladder whose first rung is planted on the ground and whose top reaches the heavens. The issue is not only how high a rung one is on but whether or not one is making an honest effort to grow and climb higher. The defining question is not simply where you are on the ladder but what direction you are moving in.

This is true for Jewish life in general and also true in the realm of kosher in particular.

QUESTION 10:

Why aren't all "natural," vegetarian and vegan restaurants kosher?

ANSWER:

What seems to be pure, vegetarian, and "natural" to one consumer may be quite unnatural to a kosher consumer. The following are some ingredients that may be found in natural and vegetarian foods:

• Oils: These can come from nonkosher fish and animals.

• Veggie bugs: Many vegetables may contain all sorts of little insects that are not problematic from a vegetarian perspective but are 100 percent nonkosher.

• Dead beetles: The highest quality red and pink dyes (carmine, carminic acid, and cochineal) are derived from the dried bodies of a beetle native only to South America and the Canary Islands.

• Gelatin: Have you seen the selection of yogurts at your local natural grocer? Well, many yogurts are made with gelatin, and gelatin comes from animals, primarily pigs.

• Mono- and diglycerides: These are widely used in many foods and are produced from both animal fats and vegetable fats. These and other animal derivatives are acceptable to most vegetarians but are not kosher.

• Emulsifiers: Many cookie doughs and icings just wouldn't be the same without emulsifiers, and many emulsifiers wouldn't be the same if they weren't an animal-based product.

• Secret "agents": Often, some ingredients in foods are not even listed on the label. This is because the Food and Drug Administration (FDA) does not require items known as "processing aids" to be listed as ingredients. Processing aids include various lubricants that keep products from sticking to processing equipment, antifoaming agents, and various other "agents." Many of these contain animal-based fatty acids.

• Flavorings: What food product *doesn't* contain "natural flavors"? These flavors can be made of over fifteen hundred various ingredients, some of which are animal derivatives. Believe it or not, some food flavorings contain civet cat secretions or extracts from the intestines of sperm whales, and cats and whales, though quite "natural," are hardly kosher.

INSIGHT:

Two hundred years from now, there may or may not still be a market for "all natural" foods. Without a doubt, however, there will certainly be a thriving market for kosher foods.

There are those who claim that Judaism is overly concerned with the "letter of the law" at the expense of the "spirit of the law." As I hope you have seen in the course of reading this book, the world of kosher is as filled with "spirit" as it is with "letter." Perhaps the reason why the observance of kosher has been around for millennia, and will doubtless be here for centuries to come, is precisely because Jews are so passionate about both the spirit and the letter of the law. And who knows, perhaps it is this dual love for both the "letter" and the "spirit" of Judaism that is an indispensible factor in the Jewish people also being an eternal people.

Chapter 7
The Best of the Rest
of the Pantry

(I) Then and Now:

A Brief History of Kosher in America

Baseball, mom, Chevrolet, and a New York kosher delicatessen—what could be more American? The truth is, kosher arrived in New York before New York did. In the early 1600s, what we call New York was then the wild, rugged, frontier town known as Dutch New Amsterdam. While some people speculate that Christopher Columbus was Jewish, to the best of our knowledge it was in New Amsterdam that the New World's first Jews arrived, and with them, the need for kosher food.

In 1654, a French ship carrying twenty-three Jews arrived in New Amsterdam, where they received a very chilly welcome from the Dutch director-general, Peter Stuyvesant. Stuyvesant, with his big black mustache, silver-tipped wooden leg, and large sword, was an intimidating figure. He ruled the town with a firm hand and wasn't interested in any citizens who weren't members of the Dutch Reformed Church. He wanted the Jews evicted, and the sooner the better. Try as he might, Stuyvesant was unable to get rid of New Amsterdam's Jews. Not only that, the Jewish settlers soon founded Congregation Shearith Israel, the Spanish and Portuguese synagogue, and in 1660 Stuyvesant's own town of New Amsterdam licensed Asher Levy as North America's first kosher butcher. Four years later, a British fleet captured New Amsterdam and the city's name was changed to New York. Peter Stuyvesant lived out the rest of his life on an island called Manhattan, the same island that would eventually be home to millions of Asher Levy's fellow Jews and dozens and dozens of kosher restaurants.

THE REST IS HISTORY

In the early days, while fruits and vegetables were readily available in New York and all households did their own baking, finding kosher meat was the biggest challenge for Jews who kept kosher. By and large, Congregation Shearith Israel was responsible for overseeing the kosher slaughtering and preparing of kosher meat for New York's Jews. As the Jewish community blossomed, so did the market for kosher meat. In eighteenth century New York, if you wanted to open a butcher shop, kosher or not, you needed a license from the city. As more and more kosher butcher shops opened, it was only a matter of time until the first complaint was registered, and it happened in 1771. The butcher's name was Moshe, better known as Moshe the Shochet, and a customer registered a formal complaint with the city questioning the reliability of Moshe's kosher meats. The first record of a kosher license being revoked is from 1796. A widow, Mrs. Hetty Hays, had accused her butcher of selling nonkosher meat as kosher. From there, it was a hop, skip, and a jump to today's world of sophisticated, professional kosher certification agencies.

BITS AND BITES OF KOSHER HISTORY

The birth of kosher supervision in America: In 1752, Congregation Shearith Israel began supervising all kosher meat slaughtering in New York City.[7]

The kosher "Queen City of the West": By 1840, Cincinnati was home to the second largest Jewish community in America. Two synagogues, Bnai Israel and Bnai Yeshurun, organized the "Cincinnati Kashruth Committee."[8]

Where science and kashrut first met: In 1842, the *Baltimore Sun* reported that some companies were mixing lard oil into olive oil and selling it as "pure olive oil." Mrs. Rebecca Esther Noah, wife of Judge Mordecai M. Noah, was outraged. Judge Noah, along with a pharmacist and a chemistry professor, developed two tests that could be used to establish the purity of olive oil, and put kosher housewives at ease.[9]

West Coast kosher: In the early 1850s, Alexander Iser published an Almanac for San Francisco that listed two kosher boarding houses, a butcher, and a matzah bakery.[10]

Confederate and kosher: In 1864, Isaac Levy, a confederate soldier from Virginia, wrote to his sister that he and his brother "purchased matzot sufficient to last for the week. The cost [in Charleston] is somewhat less than in Richmond, being but two dollars a pound. . . . We had a fine vegetable soup and a pound and a half of kosher beef, the latter sells for four dollars per pound in Charleston."[11]

From soap to nuts: In 1870, Rokeach Co. introduced its first product: kosher soap. Today hundreds of kosher food products are manufactured by Rokeach.[12]

It started with matzah: If there is one food that is absolutely vital for a Jewish diet, it's matzah. In the early 1800s, Jacob Horowitz was the first person to bake matzah commercially in America. In 1888, Dov Ber Manischewitz opened a small matzah factory in Cincinnati, Ohio. Twenty years later, the Manischewitz Company was baking over fifty thousand pounds of matzah a day to meet the demand across the country and around the world. In 1940, Manischewitz gave birth to its first nonmatzah product. Mazel tov, it's a Tam Tam.[13]

Marketing to a higher authority: In 1905, Isadore Pinkowitz, founder of Hebrew National, produced the first line of kosher hot dogs. Sixty years later, Hebrew National launched an ad campaign featuring the line "We answer to a higher authority," to market its hot dogs to the general marketplace. Isadore would have had a lot of *nachas* (pride).[14]

It's the law: In 1915, the first kosher food law in the United States was passed by the New York State Legislature. Since that time, similar laws have been passed across the country. These laws have been challenged by those who contend that they violate the establishment clause in the Constitution, though they have stood up in court.[15]

The OU: In 1924, the Union of Orthodox Jewish Congregations of America (OU), at the urging of its Women's Branch, began its work in the field of kosher supervision. This marked the beginning of a revolution for the kosher consumer in America and, indeed, around the world.[16]

Bagels and cream cheese: While the origins of the bagel are shrouded in seventeenth-century Polish legend, bagels eventually became a popular food with many European Jews, who brought their taste with them to America. Kosher bagels were being baked by kosher bakeries in the early 1900s, though the years 1927–28 represented a turning point for American Jews. In 1927, Henry Lender of West Haven, Connecticut, began mass producing bagels primarily for Jewish delicatessens in New York. And in 1928, Kraft Foods bought a small brand of cheese now known as Philadelphia cream cheese. Almost from the moment those products met, they became emblematic of American Jewish culture.[17]

The Maxwell House Haggadah: In 1930, Maxwell House launched the most effective kosher marketing effort since God gave the Torah to the Jews at Sinai. The Passover Seder is the most widely observed of all Jewish holidays, and Maxwell House coffee marketed its kosher for Passover coffee by publishing the Maxwell House Haggadah. Over the years, millions of these Haggadahs were distributed, and they became synonymous with Passover for generations of Jews.[18]

The Real Thing: To the delight of dentists everywhere, Coca-Cola went kosher in 1937. Coca-Cola now produces an annual run of Kosher for Passover Classic Coke. Coke aficionados will tell you that this is the best Coke around because it contains real sugar and not corn syrup.[19]

OK with me: The OK kosher certification agency was established in 1935. You can thank it for kosher Tropicana orange juice.[20]

The Star-K: Baltimore, Maryland, became one of the most dynamic Jewish communities in America. Baltimore was home to the second oldest synagogue in the country, to the Ner Israel Rabbinical College, and to a large observant community. In 1947, the Orthodox Jewish Council began to supervise kashrut in the city, and this service eventually grew into the Star-K. Today, the Star-K is one of the four largest and most prestigious kosher certification organizations in the world.[21]

Shabbat at Camp David: In 1977, U.S. President Jimmy Carter hosted Egyptian President Anwar Sadat and Israeli Prime Minister Menachem Begin at Camp David for historic peace talks. A completely kosher kitchen was set up to provide meals for the prime minister. Reflecting on his kosher Friday night dinner, President Carter said, "Everybody was in a good mood. I think because it was the Sabbath. Begin told me they always observed the Sabbath with rejoicing and singing."[22]

Take me out to the ballpark: In 1992, the Baltimore Orioles moved into their new stadium, Oriole Park at Camden Yards. The stadium included the first kosher food stand in the major leagues. It wasn't long until others followed.

The Kosher tundra: In 1991, Rabbi Yossi Greenberg and his wife Esty opened a Chabad House in Anchorage, Alaska. Today there is a kosher section in one of the supermarkets in Anchorage. In Ketchikan, Alaska, Steven Dulin operates a kosher bed and breakfast. He imports kosher food from Seattle.[23]

The Magic Kingdom goes kosher: To have kosher meals waiting for you at most Walt Disney World restaurants, all you need to do is call twenty-four hours ahead of time, and Mickey himself will make sure your food is waiting.

Pastrami in Witchita: Though there are only 1,000 Jews in Witchita, for the annual Deli Day celebration, they truck in kosher pastrami from Kansas City.[24]

The Star-D: In 1996, the National Council of Young Israel launched a new national kosher certification in partnership with the Star-K. The Star-D is the only national *hechsher* exclusively for dairy products.

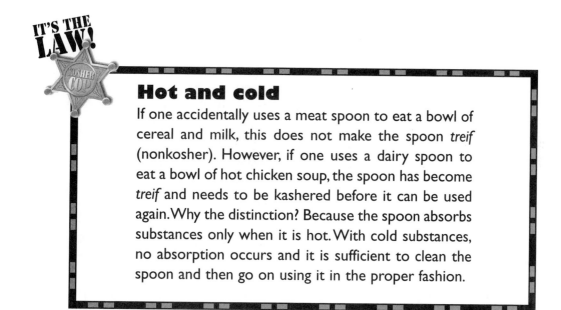

Hot and cold

If one accidentally uses a meat spoon to eat a bowl of cereal and milk, this does not make the spoon *treif* (nonkosher). However, if one uses a dairy spoon to eat a bowl of hot chicken soup, the spoon has become *treif* and needs to be kashered before it can be used again. Why the distinction? Because the spoon absorbs substances only when it is hot. With cold substances, no absorption occurs and it is sufficient to clean the spoon and then go on using it in the proper fashion.

The Oreo: The Oreo cookie went kosher in 1997. Now, if only there were peace in Israel, all would be right with the Jewish world.[25]

A kosher White House: The 2000 presidential election featured vice-presidential candidate Joseph Lieberman. Lieberman's strict observance of kashrut prompted many in the media to speculate about a Democratic victory resulting in the White House itself going kosher.

Kosher scouting: Every four years, the Boy Scouts of America hold a national jamboree. In 2001, 250 scouts received meals that were *glatt* kosher and *cholov* Yisroel. And speaking of scouts, in case you were wondering, Girl Scout cookies are kosher.[26]

Alaskan cruise: Relax in an Aqua Spa, be awed by glaciers, watch orcas, and enjoy lavish kosher dining. Since the early

1990s, there has been an explosion in kosher cruises to just about every destination imaginable.

KosherBison.com: The Internet has become the largest kosher grocery store on the planet. An endless array of kosher wines, meals, rugeluch, candies, birthday cakes, gift baskets, and more is now just a mouse click away. In 2002, KosherBison.com (http://kosherbison.com) began selling its glatt kosher, low-cholesterol products on-line and across the country.

Proud to serve: The United States military provides its soldiers with an assortment of MREs (meals ready to eat). Some of the glatt kosher MREs available to Jewish soldiers are, beef stew, chicken primavera with noodles, and cheese ravioli. During the Iraq war, when the army lost hundreds of kosher Passover meals, UPS came to the rescue and got replacement meals to the soldiers in time for a Seder that was held in Saddam Hussein's palace.[27]

Kosher for the Clueless but Curious: In 2004, in recognition of the need for a user-friendly guide to kosher, the Star-K joined with the Jewish Literacy Foundation to commission the book you are now reading.

Kosher on the moon: In the mid-1960s, kosher food was first offered as an option on airlines. In 2002, NASA provided Israeli astronaut Ilan Ramon with dehydrated kosher meals.[28] Who knows, with nongovernment companies now beginning to book private space flights, it may not be long until kosher arrives on the moon.

(II) The Adventures of a Star-K Mashgiach

Quick, what do Kodiak, Alaska and Sarong Irian Jaya, Indonesia, have in common? If you answered that both are home to fish production plants that are supervised by a globetrotting Star-K *mashgiach* by the name of Joel Weinberger, then you are absolutely correct.

[I] A "TAIL" OF TWO CITIES
JOEL WEINBERGER

Kodiak, Alaska, is known as Alaska's Emerald Isle. On Kodiak Island, lush green mountains are framed by a deep blue sky and wisps of snow-white clouds. Kodiak is famous for its huge brown bears, unparalleled sport fishing, and breathtaking beauty. The island has seven villages and is home to one of the country's largest commercial fishing ports, which is why I go there. It's my job, as a Star-K *mashgiach*, to represent the rest of the Jews in the world who want to eat Alaskan salmon but just can't make the trip themselves to Kodiak to make sure their fish is perfectly kosher.

The Alaskan salmon season is short and fickle. The salmon season lasts only six to eight weeks from July to August, and there is no guarantee that quality salmon will be caught or that the weather will cooperate. In order for me to do my job, it is vital that the quality of fish and weather conditions work in unison so that the company workers and I can also work together to successfully produce kosher salmon. Unfortunately, things don't always work the way we would like.

Getting There Is Half the Fun
Reaching the remote cannery on Kodiak is no easy task. The trip to Kodiak begins with a flight to Anchorage. From

Anchorage I take a small commuter plane to Kodiak and from there a two-seater pontoon plane that lands in the frigid waters off the island—Kodiak has no runway. In Alaska, you never know when you might run into dense fog, high winds, and lashing rain. It's not unusual for flights to be cancelled, and Mother Nature could potentially cancel the complete production run of kosher salmon. To deal with this reality, tight production schedules are not recommended. Workers, inspectors, and *mashgichim* all need to leave themselves ample time in Anchorage so that if the weather clears, they will be ready to take the flight to Kodiak at a moment's notice.

Once I arrive at the cannery, the next and most important challenge has to do with the fish themselves. Are fish available for production, and if they are, is the quality acceptable? If the weather cooperates, and if fish availability and quality issues are resolved, the cannery then has to be transformed into a Star-K kosher-approved fish production facility.

The Star-K has a highly detailed and organized system for fish plants. First and foremost, the *mashgiach* must become personally acquainted with each and every fish. Every one of the many thousands or more salmon must be checked for fins and scales. From the troller ship, the salmon enter the plant at a very rapid rate, and the *mashgiach* needs to don full fisherman's gear in order to position himself accordingly on the production line so that he can see each fish clearly. One by one, each fish is inspected, and that's just the beginning.

The next step is to make sure that all the production equipment is kosher. Conveyor belts, processing tables, racks, and retorts (huge machines that sterilize canned foods) must all undergo proper kosherization. The *mashgiach* himself must turn on the boilers and fires that steam the fish. A customized tracking system ensures that the raw salmon viewed as it entered the plant is the same product that is prepared, canned, retorted, and labeled. The *mashgiach* must also verify the flow of all ingredients from the warehouse to the factory floor. The entire process takes three to four days. In that time, tens of thousands of fish are processed, and in the end we have over ten thousand cans of Star-K-certified kosher salmon ready for shipment to grocery stores across the country. I don't leave the plant without full fish accountability, meaning I account for every can by canning code.

At the end of my five or six days on Kodiak Island, I return home for a good rest before embarking on my next adventure: to Indonesia, where I will supervise the production of tuna.

A Look at Kosher Tuna Production

Tuna production is vastly different from salmon production. A much larger volume of fish is handled and the production time tends to be much longer, up to ten or fourteen days.

Today, most tuna production takes place in the Far East, and since most tuna production runs commence on a Sunday night or Monday morning and since I lose a day when crossing the International Dateline, my departure needs to be on the Tuesday or Wednesday prior to the start of the scheduled production. I spend Shabbat at a hotel near the facility so production can start on Sunday as planned.

Before production can begin, the tuna facility must be thoroughly cleaned and then kashered. For this to run smoothly, a good relationship between the *mashgiach* and the entire staff is imperative. Successful cleaning and kashering can be achieved only if there is a spirit of cooperation and coordination. You would be amazed at how proficient hundreds of Indonesian factory workers have become in carrying out all the details Jewish law requires in the kashering process.

The butchering knives, carts, tables, fill lines, holding tanks, cookers, and baskets all need to be cleaned and kashered. To clean them we dip each and every item in a caustic solution, and to kasher them we either immerse each item in boiling water or place them in a steam chamber.

The production process then begins by dividing the tuna into species: albacore, skipjack, tongol, or yellow fin. Each variety is produced separately. The variety selected for production is defrosted, sized, and brought to the first set of work tables. The fish is inspected by the *mashgiach* and then gutted, cleaned, and steamed. After gutting and steaming, the tuna goes into a cooking chamber, where it is misted and cooled rapidly. This facilitates the skinning and cleaning of the fish. Once the fish is skinned and the head has been removed, the tuna is ready to be packed. Very clean tuna loins are categorized as "solid white" or "solid light," depending on the species of tuna. Tuna pieces coming off the cutting machine are commonly known as "chunk white" or "chunk light." Scraps and dark scrapings are canned as cat food. (It's amazing how many cats keep kosher these days without even realizing it.)

Myths & Facts

Myth: Giraffe is technically a kosher animal, but since it is impossible for a *shochet* to know where on the giraffe's neck to make the cut, in practice there has never been a piece of kosher giraffe meat.

Fact: Giraffe is kosher, and it is also known where on the giraffe a *shochet* needs to cut. The reason you will find bison burgers and not giraffe burgers at your kosher butcher is purely a question of economics. There is just no cost-effective manner of capturing, slaughtering, and processing giraffe meat. Besides, the demand is not very great—yet.

In addition to supervising this entire process, the *mashgiach* must ensure that the steam that heats other cooking equipment in a different area of the plant is not captured and recycled through the factory to the area where the Star-K production is taking place. Steam from a nonkosher product can render the kosher tuna unfit. This concern for complete plant segregation applies not only to steam, ovens, and equipment, but to the workers' personal equipment, especially their filleting knives. For Star-K productions, care must be taken to ensure that workers don't take their knives home. We make sure to keep these kosher knives under lock and key in the facility.

Finally, another safeguard common to both salmon and tuna canning is encoding the cans with production codes indicating they were processed under Star-K supervision. All canning productions emboss or laser print production codes on the tops of the cans. When the Star-K supervises a fish production, additional letters, or the word *Star-K*, are added to the production code. When the cans are ready to be labeled, the *mashgiach* can easily check that the correct products are being labeled with the Star-K symbol.

In the near future, Cambodia and Vietnam will be moving into the tuna processing business. Regardless of where my job takes me, I will always consider it a privilege to be part of a worldwide team dedicated to ensuring the highest standards of kashrut for the consumers who depend on us.

[II] HOTEL CALIFORNIA
YAEL KANER

Many of the most memorable moments of my life have only been possible because I am a *mashgiach* and work in the kosher catering business. I've catered kosher events at the Supreme Court, the White House, and Bally's casino in Atlantic City. I catered a kosher event hosted by the vice president of one of the world's largest high-tech companies where the entertainment was provided by In Sync. I've met Bill Clinton, Elie Weisel, and

Rudy Giuliani, all at kosher events, and I did the catering for the Bar Mitzvah of Steven Spielberg's nephew, where I met Mr. Dreamworks himself. I even catered a Pre-Passover Seder for the Dalai Lama. So what's it like to do a big kosher event in a hotel, convention center, private mansion, or casino? It's awesome. It's also a huge amount of work and an enormous responsibility, but what can I say, I love it.

The following is an overview of the major steps that go into making sure that something like a foreign embassy dinner reception or a Ritz Carlton wedding are 100 percent kosher.

The Food Arrives

One week before a big event, the nonperishable goods begin to arrive at the catering kitchen. This can easily be dozens of products in lots and lots of boxes. My first job is to make sure that all the products have kosher certification. It's not uncommon for 5–10 percent of the products to be returned because they weren't kosher. How could that happen? Simple. Let's say I'm dealing with an order for three cases of paprika and the warehouse only has two. The salesperson or the warehouse supervisor might not know that there is such a thing as non-kosher paprika, and in his desire to properly fill the order, he sends me two boxes of paprika with a *hechsher* and one without. If that one box slips through and ends up as seasoning for a few dozen chickens, I have a huge problem on my hands.

The Bok Choy Arrives

Once the fresh produce arrives, it all needs to be checked for those little bugs that many consumers would never notice, but that it's my job to make sure to notice. Because while strawberries, bock choy, baby spinach, and cabbage are all kosher, the bugs that like to hide on them aren't. Each fruit and vegetable has its own specific checking procedure that was designed to hunt down and eliminate the bugs that like to call that particular item home.

Three Chefs, One Mashgiach

In addition to being a *mashgiach,* I also happen to be a chef, and that is very helpful. A *mashgiach* working in a large, busy kitchen needs to develop a kind of sixth sense that enables him to "smell" kashrut issues even before they arise. As a chef, I have the benefit of having a hands-on feel for exactly what takes place in the kitchen.

The kitchen staff for a large event will often include a chef, a sous chef, a pastry chef, two to three kitchen helpers, and at least one dishwasher. That's a lot of fast-working hands to keep an eye on. To give you one example of the interaction between the *mashgiach* and chefs, consider the pastry chef. It is the responsibility of the *mashgiach* to personally crack open and then check every egg for blood spots. For a large event, this can mean many dozen or even many hundreds of eggs. And while I'm cracking and inspecting those eggs, my sixth sense needs to be on the alert for potential problems elsewhere in the kitchen. If I spot a problem, or if one of the other chefs has a question they need to discuss, then the pastry chef has to wait while I make sure everything is okay. Or should I say, Star-K.

A Makeshift Kitchen At the Ritz

In some large cities like Los Angeles, Washington DC, and New York there are hotels with their own kosher kitchens. The *mashgiach* literally holds the keys to these kitchens. When not in use, the kosher kitchen is locked and the only person with a key to it is the *mashgiach.* Not even the hotel manager has a key.

In a hotel where there is no kosher kitchen, or at a special venue like a symphony hall, art museum, or private home where there is going to be a kosher wedding, seminar, bar mitzvah, or luncheon, the caterer will need to set up a makeshift kitchen.

Let me tell you a little about what takes place behind the scenes of a kosher event in a hotel without a kosher kitchen. First, we need to bring in everything. Cookers and warmers, pots and pans, dinnerware and silverware; absolutely everything. Then we construct our kitchen in one of the back hallways of the hotel. (And believe me, it's always stuffy back there.) These events often call for more than one *mashgiach* because there needs to be a *mashgiach* at every entrance to the kitchen to inspect every food item that is brought in. Of course, everything I mentioned earlier about the chefs, the bok choy, and the sixth sense all happen at a hotel event. Additionally, since it is the hotel's waiters and waitresses that work these events, they need to be monitored so that no one brings nonkosher snacks into the kitchen area. Also, since the hotel staff is accustomed to working in their regular kitchen, it often happens that if they can't locate a certain utensil in the makeshift kosher kitchen, like a spatula or a mixing bowl, that they will innocently borrow one from the *treif* hotel kitchen, and that can be a big problem.

The bar is another area that needs to be monitored at a kosher hotel event. Every case and every bottle of wine and liquor needs to be inspected by the *mashgiach* before it is used. The same is true with the condiments at the bar; they all need to be checked. This is another area where the hotel staff could make an innocent mistake. Let's say the bartender runs out of maraschino cherries; what does he do? He can't leave the bar, and he certainly doesn't want to serve certain drinks without a cherry, so he will ask one of the waitresses to go get a few bottles of cherries. The waitress will then run over to one of the other hotel banquet halls, grab a few bottles from under the bar, and bring them to the bartender. One problem; there is no *hechsher* on those cherries. Bottom line: you have be on your toes at all times.

Finally, you want to know when the *mashgiach* goes home? When the last fork is cleared. After all the guests have left. After all the tables have been cleared. After everything is packed and checked and loaded onto a truck—then the *mashgiach* can go home for the night.

Penguin eggs

As a rule, nonkosher animals produce nonkosher products. This explains why chicken eggs are kosher but penguin and turtle eggs are not. The same is true for milk. Pig milk is just as treif as pork. The exception to the rule is honey; bees are not kosher, but honey is.

[III] THE CHOCOLATE, VANILLA, STRAWBERRY MASHGIACH
DON MOSCOVITZ

It's a beautiful, crisp Monday morning and I'm on my way to a flavor company where I work for the Star-K. For a *mashgiach*, Mondays are the busiest day of the week. Monday is when we make sure that everything in the plant is ready for the upcoming week. There is often a lot of equipment that needs to be kashered before work can begin.

I enjoy the challenge of making sure that a huge plant that supplies flavors for hundreds of products that will be eaten by thousands and thousands of people is 100 percent ready to go. My window is down as I approach the plant, I can hear the sounds of the birds singing, petunias have begun to bloom, and I'm ready for work.

My first order of business is to don a customized uniform that is necessary because of an array of sanitary, quality control, and safety issues. In addition to special pants and a shirt, I have safety glasses, slip-proof steel-toed shoes, hair net, beard net, hard hat, and lab coat. Once I've dressed, I assess what needs to be done and create a plan of action. To do this, I begin by checking the last entry into the Rabbi's Journal that was made by the *mashgiach* who was last on duty Saturday night. We can never overdo communication.

Meet the Spray Driers

I soon determine that I have three tanks to check for heat, four batch makers that need my attention, an investigation of a suspicious ingredient to complete, and a spray drier to kasher. Of these, the spray drier takes precedence because production is at an absolute standstill until it is kashered. This spray drier is a four-story-tall combination of tanks and pipes that is used to convert liquids into powder. The spray drier needs kashering because last week it was used in the manufacturing of a nonkosher flavor. Since its last use, the spray drier was cleaned, inspected by a *mashgiach*, spot cleaned again with cold water while a *mashgiach* supervised, was then sealed and locked by a mashgiach for twenty-four hours, and is now ready for kashering.

Kashering a spray drier is a formidable task. There is a specific procedure that needs to be carefully implemented to ensure the kashering process is perfect. There are many types of spray driers and each requires the creation of its own kashering protocol. In general terms, the kashering process consists of a combination of dowsing all the chambers and surface areas within the tanks, and all the pipes connected to them, with boiling water and dry heat. And there is a specific order in which this needs to be done. If there was a weather report for kashering a spray drier, it would sound like this: Rain today, heavy at times, with periods of hot rain. Temperature, a clammy 87 degrees. Fog vapors will permeate the air, with thunder-like rumblings accompanied by deafening intermittent hissing. Visibility will be less than twenty feet. Humidity, one hundred percent.

When all goes well, the kashering takes three to four hours. Steam, however, tends to wreak havoc on the mechanical-electrical system, and we often need reinforcements from the plant maintenance department.

Supervision, Records, and Labels

Some companies have a *mashgiach* who only visits a few times a month, but this particular flavor company employs a *mashgiach t'midi*, a "continuous supervision *mashgiach*." The plant operates seven days a week, twenty-four hours a day. In essence, we live here. There are three of us who work in shifts that cover almost ninety hours a week. We also have a back-up *mashgiach* who is on call when the company needs extra coverage. During the hours that we are not in the plant, the company is only allowed to process batches that contain no kosher-sensitive ingredients. For this reason, all ingredients that arrive at the receiving department must have a kosher certification letter on file. In addition to the certification letter, we also get support from Star-K headquarters, where there is detailed information on every ingredient used in the plant. The system we have in place enables us to check ingredients both before and after production. Additionally, everything in the entire plant is labeled kosher, nonkosher, pareve, or dairy.

In addition to the *mashgiach*, plant employees also need to be on their toes. Each batchmaker is trained to know that when a kosher-sensitive ingredient needs to be added to a batch, that he must call the *mashgiach* and use the ingredient only while the *mashgiach* is present. For this reason, when I arrived this morning, I had four batch makers waiting for me. When I supervise the use of a kosher-sensitive ingredient, I fill out forms that record the date, time, product number, lot number, manufacturer, quantity made, packaging, and customer name. Talk about paperwork! But wait, there is more. Each flavor produced, and each jug, carton, tote, or drum filled with the product, must be labeled and signed by the *mashgiach*. It isn't uncommon for me to sign hundreds of labels per shift. Each label is numbered and recorded and great care is taken to sign only the exact amount of labels needed. We don't want any chance of an extra kosher label ending up on the wrong container of flavoring. I monitor how many containers are actually used, any extra labels are returned directly to me for destruction, and the number of destroyed labels is also recorded.

Beyond the Spray Driers

This flavor company has over one hundred vessels that are used to measure, weigh, and manufacture products. These include tanks, pots, beakers, cups, and more. Many of the tanks have fixed mixers in them, and for others there are portable mixers on wheels. There are also rubber and plastic pumps and hoses that, according to Star-K standards, can't be kashered. We have a system for tracking the status—kosher, nonkosher, dairy or pareve—of each tank, mixer, vessel, pump, and hose. Each is permanently marked, and in case there is a failure in the tracking system, we have a back-up system in place. All of these items need careful supervision when heat is introduced into them. If there is a nonkosher ingredient present when heat is introduced, we have a problem on our hands. For this reason, the *mashgiach* needs to be alerted whenever heat is used.

Finally, I have an investigation to do today. It seems that one batch maker manufactured a flavor that yielded an amount of product greater than the sum of the ingredients required. As far as I know, only God can create something from nothing, so until I can verify that nothing nonkosher was used, I simply can't certify that batch. At this point, it's up to the company to trace every ingredient used in the batch and to provide me with a thorough accounting.

At the End of the Day

This is a cursory look at some of the activities involved in my day. A detailed description could literally fill a book. You may be wondering if my supervision procedures are perfect in every way. Of course perfection is elusive, but at the end of the day, I am more than happy with the job I've done. I know that our standards of supervision and certification go well beyond the minimum of what Jewish law requires and thus ensures that if there have been any mistakes, our flavors will still be well within accepted standards of kashrut. And so, as I travel home on a cool Monday evening, I feel good about the job I have done to ensure that Jews around the world will eat kosher.

(III) Bottom Line:
Is This a "Good *Hechsher*"?

At times, we all wish that life were simpler than it is, but usually that's just not the way things work. The contemporary world of kosher food certification is one such example. Let's step back and imagine for a moment what kosher certification is actually all about. We'll begin by reflecting on an era now long gone.

WHEN MOM RULED THE KITCHEN

Once upon a time, just about everything a person ate was made, from scratch, by someone in the family, usually Mom. In such a world, mom *was* the *hechsher*. Keeping a kosher home was very important to Mom. She was wellversed in the laws relating to preparing and cooking kosher food, and if she ever had a question she would simply ask the local rabbi. In those days, about the only part Mom didn't do herself was slaughter meat and fowl. For that, she relied on the local *shochet* who was always a learned and respected member of the community. Between Mom, the *shochet*, and the local rabbi, just about every issue related to kosher food consumption was covered.

Back in Mom's kitchen, things were fairly simple, and then one day, the world began to change. Soon, multibillion-dollar companies such as Nestlé, Procter and Gamble, Nabisco, Coca-Cola, ConAgra, Quaker Oats, Domino, Kraft, Hershey, Heinz, and Kellogg's, and everybody else who thought they knew how to cook as well as Mom, also wanted you to trust their commitment to kosher the same way you trusted Mom's. It wasn't long until the local rabbi was swamped with requests from dozens of corporate CEOs, each of whom wanted him to assure the world of kosher consumers that their goodies were just as kosher as Mom's. As you can imagine, the rabbi soon became overwhelmed, kosher moms everywhere became bewildered, and millions of kosher consumers had questions about whether or not Mrs. Heinz and Mr. Kraft were as careful with their observance of kosher as mom and the local rabbi were.

Thus was born the kosher certification industry, more or less. You see, as food production became more and more commercialized, and as the demand for kosher food mushroomed, it became necessary that literally thousands of people be involved in the process of ensuring that foods that declared themselves to be kosher actually were. These people not only had to serve as surrogates for Mom and the local rabbi, but they needed to be much more. They needed to be as concerned about kosher food as Mom was and as well-versed in the intricate laws of kosher as the rabbi was, and on top of that, they needed to become experts in horticulture, chemistry, cutting-edge food technologies, and virtually every area of the food manufacturing industry. And keep in mind, the food industry produces more products than the automobile and computer industries combined.

WOULDN'T IT BE NICE

For kosher consumers, it would be ideal if there were just one kosher certification organization and that any item bearing the symbol of that organization was 100 percent reliably kosher.

The reality, however, is that with the explosion in demand for kosher food, enormous growth occurred in the number of organizations and individuals that function as kosher certifiers within the food industry. On the one hand, this is a boon for the kosher consumer because it means that hardly a week passes that a new kosher food product doesn't come on the market. At the same time, as in any large industry, it can also give rise to confusion, problems, and even abuse.

Today, well over seven hundred kosher certification organizations exist in the world. Some of these are staffed by just one rabbi who may supervise only one or two products, some have a small staff, and others may employ dozens and even hundreds of rabbis and other support staff.

In actuality, just a handful of kosher certification agencies oversee the kosher standards of the majority of food products manufactured by the largest companies in the food industry. If you venture into your local grocery store and begin to examine the national-brand products bearing a kosher certification symbol, by and large you will find that the great majority of items are endorsed by one of the major kosher agencies. At the same time, an ever-increasing number of items—in fact, thousands of items—are under the supervision of smaller agencies. The fact that an agency is small, even as small as a one-person operation, has no bearing on whether or not it does an excellent job at kosher certification. It's just that with so many people and so many products involved, it's inevitable that issues and concerns will arise.

The bottom line is, in the world of contemporary kosher food, "Is this a good *hechsher*?" is a prevalent, relevant, and tricky question.

WHAT EXACTLY IS THE QUESTION?
The question of reliability in kosher food supervision essentially comes down to four issues:

1. Orthodox and nonorthodox kosher standards: The majority of those who carefully observe the laws of kashrut are orthodox Jews. In the nonorthodox community, while many members consider kosher very important, the laws that govern kashrut are different. Practically speaking, some foods that are not considered kosher according to orthodox law would be regarded as kosher in the conservative or reform community. For this reason, a consumer who wants to eat only food that is considered kosher by orthodox standards must know whether or not the rabbi or agency behind a particular *hechsher* is orthodox.

2. Two Jews, three opinions: Every area of Jewish law seems to elicit a range of scholarly opinions regarding the manner in which certain laws are applied. This is also the case with regard to the laws of kashrut. Within orthodox rabbinic circles, various opinions are expressed about what is or isn't necessary to ensure that a commercially manufactured food item meets the strictest application of Jewish law. The result is that some agencies may follow one set of guidelines while others may follow a slightly modified set of guidelines. For consumers who want their personal observance of kashrut to adhere to a particular scholarly view, it becomes vital to know which guidelines any given *hechsher* represents, and this can get confusing.

3. Non-Jewish kosher consumer factor: Jews are no longer the only consumers of kosher food. Vegetarians rely on the presence of a *hechsher* to tell them they are definitely not eating meat, Muslims buy kosher meat because *shechita* satisfies Islamic slaughtering requirements, doctors regularly tell patients with lactose intolerance that certain kosher foods are reliably dairy free, Seventh-Day Adventists look for kosher food for religious reasons, vegans know that kosher means no animal byproducts,

and millions of other people believe that the presence of a *hechsher* automatically means the presence of higher standards of nutrition and cleanliness. The fact that so many consumers beyond just the traditional Jewish market see added value in foods that are certified kosher motivates companies to produce kosher products. The good news is that more and more companies are seeking kosher certification. The bad news is that leniencies in Jewish law that concern many Jews who keep kosher are of no concern to the rest of the kosher market. This creates a tricky situation where it is possible to have kosher supervision that is *technically* kosher though not up to the highest standards of much of the Jewish kosher market. Those who want only kosher foods that adhere to the highest standards must know the procedures and guidelines followed by individual agencies and rabbis.

4. Fraud: Though this rarely happens, in some instances unscrupulous individuals have presented themselves to companies as being reputable certifiers of kosher products when in fact they weren't. Knowing that companies are always looking to keep costs down, they charge a fee substantially lower than the reputable agencies and require the bare minimum from the manufacturer in terms of additional labor and equipment costs.

For all of these reasons, it is always valid for someone who keeps kosher to ask, "Is this a good *hechsher*?" "Good," in this instance, means that the rabbis who are responsible for the *hechsher* apply the standards you desire. How does one ascertain which halachic standards any given rabbi or agency applies? The only way to know is if the rabbis themselves tell you. In almost all cases they already have, and it's just a matter of doing a little research.

There are a few easy ways to find out if a *hechsher* is up to your standards.

  1. Almost all of the very large, well-known certifying agencies apply the standards that are sought after by those who are most concerned with the strictest application of Jewish law. These regional, national, and international agencies include, but are certainly not limited to, the following—

 The Star-K

 "OU" Union of Orthodox Jewish Congregations

 "Circle K" Organized Kashruth Laboratories

 "COR" Kashruth Council of Toronto

 "OV" Vaad Hoeir of St. Louis

 London Beth Din

2. It's impossible to list all of the national, regional, and local certifying agencies here. The easiest thing to do, especially if you are just beginning to keep kosher, is to ask the rabbi or coach who is helping you through the process which agencies adhere to your standards and which don't.

3. If you have a question about an agency or a particular product, you can call the Star-K hotline: (410) 484-4110.

4. *Kashrus Magazine* publishes an annual list of almost every kosher certification agency in the world, along with contact information and information about the rabbis responsible for determining their standards. Some other very good sources of information about kosher agencies and products are:

   http://www.kashrut.com

   http://www.oukosher.org

   http://www.star-k.org

   http://www.kashrusmagazine.com

   http://www.kosherquest.org

   http://www.koshertoday.com

(IV) Kosher Travel and Kosher in-a-Pinch

The first thing the novice kosher traveler needs to do is relax. Unless you are planning to spend a week with your family in an exotic place like Curaçao, you will have little trouble keeping kosher on your next vacation. (And if you do happen to be traveling to Curaçao, give me a call because I know a wonderful family there that keeps kosher and would be more than happy to help you out.)

Let's begin with some general information:

1. Big City, USA: Most larger cities in the United States and Canada, as well as Europe, have at least one kosher restaurant. Many of these cities also have a kosher grocery store. Before your trip, contact the local *vaad hakashrut*. A *vaad* is a rabbinic organization that is responsible for local kosher establishments, such as restaurants, bakeries, and caterers. Your family rabbi or your own local *vaad* should be able to give you contact information for just about any community in the country. Next, and this might be the most practical step of all, play the game of "Jewish Geography." In this game, you do some networking among friends to find out who has a friend or relative that keeps kosher in the city you will be visiting. Give that person a call and he or she will be able to tell you everything you need to know in ten minutes or less.

2. Grocery stores: Remember, virtually the same kosher products that are available in your local grocery store will be available in any major chain store in the country.

3. Hotel concierge: If you will be staying in a hotel with a concierge service, the concierge will probably be able to direct you to local kosher restaurants. If the concierge doesn't know, he or she will be happy to do some research for you; after all, that's the concierge's job. Restaurants will gladly fax their menu to your hotel concierge and, for a fee, will deliver your dinner to the front desk.

4. Rest areas: Most turnpike rest stops feature some kind of a minimart. It's always fun to see how many items you can find in these stores that have a *hechsher*. The same is

true for the food markets that are attached to many gas stations; they are just brimming with kosher items.

5. The trusty old cooler: If you will be away from a large city, the two items that are the hardest to find are kosher meat and kosher cheese. You may need to bring these in a cooler, and don't forget to replenish the ice once a day. Also, your local butcher can probably vacuum seal any prepared meats for you to take on the road.

In a sense, the very first request God made of mankind was to keep kosher. He told Adam and Eve that it was permissible to eat from all trees but that the tree of knowledge of good and evil was strictly off-limits. Kabbalah teaches that the act of eating from the forbidden tree wreaked great havoc on the spiritual fabric of all creation. The only way to rectify this damage would be through eating. Eating kosher food, eating with an awareness of God, eating to bring goodness into the world and eating only after carefully uttering the holy words of a blessing all serve to repair the damage done when the first human beings ate what they should not have.

6. Motel kosher: It's the middle of the night, you've been driving for nine hours, your eyes are closing, you spot a sign for three hotels at the next exit, and the only problem is you have no food with you. Don't worry. At the very, very least, your motel will have vending machines

containing a few items you can eat and drink. In the morning, a kosher breakfast may be served in the lobby. The popular continental breakfast will almost always have fresh fruit, a few brands of kosher cereal, coffee, milk, plastic utensils, and—if you are lucky—prepackaged kosher frozen bagels and singleserve containers of cream cheese.

7. In a pinch: If you can survive on Mountain Dew, bottled water, pretzels, candy bars, granola bars, Planters peanuts, and bananas, then there is just about no limit to where you can spend a day and have plenty to eat. The tackle shop at some remote lake—no problem. A quaint little town with lots of cozy antique shops on Main Street but no Jews for a hundred miles—simple. An amusement park that won't allow outside food—well, if you can handle the rides, you can probably also handle a day of little more than soda, candy, and ice cream bars.

In short, with a bit of planning, and sometimes even without any planning, keeping kosher is little or no obstacle to having a great travel experience anywhere, anytime.

The following article is from the Star-K website.

ON THE ROAD TO A KOSHER VACATION
RABBI TZVI ROSEN, STAR-K KASHRUS ADMINISTRATOR; EDITOR, KASHRUS KURRENTS

Summertime is a season synonymous with travel, vacation, the great outdoors—and experiencing the heartbeat of America. A universal question that crosses the mind of every kosher vacationer is, "Is there anything kosher to eat out there?" The answer is yes, more than you think, but it is still wise to plan before your journey.

Today, kosher certifications abound on numerous convenience foods. It is refreshing to stop at a roadside store and find an assortment of crackers, cheese, snack foods, juices, beverages, and ice cream, all reliably kosher approved. Stopping to shop at your destination's supermarket will uncover all the nationally known, popular kosher-certified products that dot the shelves coast to coast.

Recently, what has emerged in the supermarkets in terms of newly found kosher approved products is a variety of kosher-frozen foods that have gained national popularity. Bagels are the most ubiquitous example. Furthermore, a supermarket's private label house brands frequently bear reliable kosher certification. Private-label products run the gamut from apple juice to canned vegetables. House-brand private labels bear kosher certification because a kosher symbol is perceived as an additional set of eyes on the product. Hence, cereals, cookies, and crackers often bear reliable supervision. In every situation, a very unusual product bearing kosher certification should always give one pause.

At times, chain supermarkets have a kosher food section even in their outlying stores because of branch stores located in Jewish neighborhoods. In other smaller communities, supermarkets may have a special "super-kosher" food section to accommodate their entire Jewish clientele. For example, a supermarket in Oklahoma City carries a complete line of glatt meats and *cholov* Yisroel cheeses. You never know where you will find a kosher section in a grocery store, so it always pays to look.

Even an overnight motel stay can be a pleasant surprise to the kosher traveler. Continental breakfasts have become very popular in most motels. These meals range from simple juice and coffee to an elegant repast of rolls, cereals, bagels, fruit, and pastries. What has made these continental breakfasts so popular with the kosher traveler is the widespread use of portion-controlled products. These individually wrapped products, known as PCs, include bagels, cereals, cream cheese, jellies, and creamers that more often than not display a hechsher right on the portion pack.

When planning a family vacation, a good idea would be to place a call to the local *vaad hakashrus*, or the community rabbi. Ask if any local brands of dairy products, baked goods, breads, or restaurants are available in the local area that are reliably kosher. Are there local or national ice cream, frozen yogurt, or donut franchises that may be certified kosher by the local *vaad*? Of course, each community has its own kashrut standards, some very reliable, others very lenient. Travelers should check with their local rabbi to see if the kashrut standards where they are going meet their own personal standards.

All in all, with a little pretravel homework, high marks can be scored in the kosher vacationing department!

(V) The Star-K: Past, Present, and Future

YOU'VE COME A LONG WAY, STAR-K!
MARGIE PENSAK

Back in 1976, the fledgling Star-K (then called the Vaad Hakashrus of Baltimore) operated out of an empty synagogue classroom. One rabbi, one part-time secretary, and one part-time executive director completed the paid staff. The not-for-profit kosher agency certified about 25 establishments, consisting mostly of local caterers, bakeries, butcher shops, and restaurants. It published *Kashrus Kurrents*, which educated the Baltimore kosher consumer about the latest developments in the world of kashrut. Their kosher hot line operated between the hours of 10 a.m. to 12 p.m. Monday through Thursday, answering questions from both kosher consumers and purveyors around the world.

FAST FORWARD TWENTY-NINE YEARS

With its corporate office based in Baltimore, the Star-K now operates satellite offices in Israel, China, Australia, India, and, closer to home, in New York, New Jersey, and California. In fact, Star-K rabbis can be found around the world supervising the "catch of the day"—everything from tuna in the tropical Fiji Island waters to herring in icy Icelandic waters. (Not to mention salmon in Alaska and Nile perch on the Ivory Coast!) They travel to Pakistan to supervise date production, to Iran for raisin production, and to Thailand for pineapple production. They supervise runs of grape juice in balmy Johannesburg and pomegranate juice in the dry, semi-arid steppes of Azerbaijan. They also put their familiar Star-K logo on slivovitz distilled in Croatia, cocoa processed in Belgium, food chemicals and herbal extracts manufactured in China, and cattle and poultry slaughtered in Mexico. Parisienne wines, Vietnamese spices, Grecian and Turkish pickled products, Moroccan olive oil, Indian oleoresins, and Russian parchment paper also bear the big Star-K.

To date, Star-K certifies 40,274 products, in over one thousand three hundred locations, in fifty-two countries around the world. Since a large percentage of these companies manufacture food chemicals and other basic ingredients used by other food companies, there is a good chance that some of the food you ate today contained flavors, acidulants, artificial sweeteners, or seasonings certified by Star-K.

A SYMBOL APART

What makes the Star-K so unique amongst the major kashrut agencies? First and foremost, all kashrut related matters are the sole responsibility of its Rabbinic Administrator, Rabbi Moshe Heinemann, who has stood at its helm since its inception. The rabbinic staff answers directly, and only, to Rabbi Heinemann. Its position as a nonprofit lay organization further strengthens the hand of its Rabbinic Administrator, by not presenting conflicts of interest which might compromise its high kashrut standards.

In addition to kosher supervision, the Star-K expends a tremendous amount of time and energy on promoting kashrut through education and research. Since its inception, consumer education has always been a hallmark of the Star-K. To this end, as a public service to kosher consumers the world over, the Star-K makes available its research on kashrut and the observance of other mitzvot (Jewish laws), through various media.

YOUR PERSONAL KOSHER TRAINER

Yes, the Star-K has evolved into a premier kosher education agency, as well! The Star-K Kosher Hot Line, (410) 484-4110, now operates 9 a.m. to 5 p.m. EST, Monday through Thursday, Friday, from 9 a.m. to closing time, depending on the season. (Until 4 p.m., during the summer months, and until 2 p.m. during the winter months.) With world renowned expertise, running the gamut from pharmaceuticals and nutritional supplements to "Sabbath mode appliances", it responds to hundreds of telephone inquiries posed by people living throughout the United States, and from as far away as England, Israel, South America, South Africa, and Australia, regarding the observance of all mitzvot, not only kashrut.

That's why on the Star-K website, www.star-k.org, you can find out not just about kosher products, but in-depth reasons for many other Jewish practices, as well. The picture of the cutesy cow standing with a child drinking a cup of milk on Star-K's homepage says it all: "Discover the World of Kosher...It's not just about milk and meat." More than just a clever take on kashrut, it depicts the uniqueness of the Star-K. Kosher food product lists, kosher consumer alerts, FAQs (Frequently Asked Questions), Comments and Questions, and current and archival editions of its newsletter, *Kashrus Kurrents*, are featured on the website.

Star-K's *Kashrus Kurrents* has grown from a small, local kashrut informational "sheet", to a first class publication distributed and read throughout the United States and beyond. Its up-to-date researched lists of kosher products are widely reproduced with permission in other magazines, synagogue and school bulletins, and websites offering kashrut information. Examples of some favorite lists include: Kosher Liquor and Liqueurs, Slurpees, Soft Drinks, Over-the-Counter Medicines, and Cereals. Kashrus Kurrent's comprehensive articles address such topics as: kosher travel; vitamins, nutritional supplements and homeopathic remedies; cosmetics and their Sabbath usage; guidelines for food products grown/produced in Israel; Passover preparations; kitchen appliances; microwaving in the workplace; vegetable checking; and, feeding your pets. *Kashrus Kurrents* articles and lists are available for view on its website, www.star-k.org, by clicking on Kosher Consumer, Kashrus Articles.

Each year the Star-K publishes its popular Passover Directory which includes the agency's Kosher for Passover Product Guide, in the interest of disseminating this information to as wide an audience as possible, in an easy-to-use, low-cost format. This oft quoted resource includes a complete guide to Passover medicines and cosmetics, based on the extensive research of Rabbi Gershon Bess of Kollel Los Angeles, as well as several comprehensive informational articles about the holiday.

Star-K's annual, complimentary, week long, Kashrus Training Seminar is just one forum in which present and future community leaders can have a hands-on, interactive Kosher learning experience. It affords them the opportunity to go behind the scenes of a first class luxury hotel's kosher kitchen, kosher manufacturing plants, a slaughterhouse, restaurant, butcher shop and bakery, in preparation for them to administer, or even pioneer a communal kosher certification agency.

Keeping You Kurrent is the Star-K's monthly public service bulletin which announces new kosher establishments and kashrut alerts. And, to help the kashrut professional stay informed, Star-K periodically distributes *Kashrus Konnections*. This is a compilation of policies meant for those in the field, although it often addresses issues that are of interest to the kosher consumer. Both publications are available via the Star-K website.

Taking its knowledge on the road, Star-K sponsors a National Kashrus Lecture Series. Drawing on the vast experience and expertise of its in-house rabbinic kashrut administrators, its speakers bureau presents seminars on a variety of topics of kashrut interest. Discussion is invited after free lectures on such topics as: Kashrus on the Rocks: An Analysis of Wine, Whiskey and Beer; Medicines and Vitamins: Kashrus Issues and Shabbos Usage; and, Shabbos and Yom Tov Appliances: The Newest Ovens and Refrigerators.

LOOKING AHEAD

Having grown tremendously in size and scope, today's Star-K budget is met almost exclusively from fees charged to certified establishments. It is in the financial position of being able to make grants to some worthy institutions, and has the luxury of being able to devote itself to projects that do not generate any revenue, but are nevertheless of vital interest to the world of kosher consumers. Its rabbinic staff is sufficiently large so as not to be over-burdened with caring only for fee paying companies. In fact, Star-K often consults and even subsidizes nursing homes, university kosher dining programs, and other public institutions that cannot afford a full-time mashgiach (kashrut supervisor), so that even if they do not have an official certification status, they can still offer their clientele kosher meals.

The book you are reading, *Kosher for the Clueless but Curious*, was commissioned by the Star-K to further our mission of educating the public about "all things kosher."

In recognition of the fact that the Star-K is so involved in promoting widespread kosher observance and education, the agency has recently been awarded a generous grant from McDonald's. Numerous educational projects on the Star-K horizon—enabled by that grant—will serve to further its mandate as a premier kosher education agency.

A practical, hands-on, interactive course in kitchen kashrut, soon to be offered on Star-K Online (www.star-k.org), is just one such project. It allows you to ask those burning questions (pun intended!) about everything you wanted to know about kosher but you were unsure of whom to ask. For example, can you ignore that drop of milk that happened to spill into that pot of spaghetti and meatballs you left uncovered on your stove top? Can you eat those hotdogs or that eggplant parmigiana that you absentmindedly placed alongside one another to cook in your oven? What do you do about that dairy fork with which you stirred your surprise gourmet anniversary dinner of Chicken Shiraz with Porcini and Whole Shallots? What do you do with the meat pot in which it was prepared? Can the dairy fork and meat pot be kosherized? Can you even eat that Chicken Shiraz with Porcini and Whole Shallots, or do you have to go to Plan B—dine out in your favorite local kosher restaurant (assuming you are lucky enough to have one, and if so, that reservations are not required when it's not a slow night)?

Take advantage of Star-K's Online kashrut course and all of Star-K's wonderful present and future opportunities to explore the World of Kosher. They are all sure to satisfy your curiosity about kosher so you will never be clueless about kashrut again!

Works Cited

1. Charles Fishman, "The Anarchist's Cookbook," Fast Company, July 2004

2. Willow Lawson, "Fighting Crime with Nutrition," Psychology Today, March/April 2003

3. Natural Ovens Bakery, http://www.naturalovens.com/Better Health/Scientific Articles

4. Ted Nugent, interview on CNN News, "Crossfire," http://www.tednugent.com

5. Leona Reynolds-Zayak, "Kosher Trends in the Canadian Kosher Market," Agri-Processing Branch, Alberta Agriculture, Food and Rural Development, March 2004 (see also http://www.koshertoday.com for related articles)

6. I. M. Levinger, Shechita in the Light of the Year 2000 (Jerusalem: Maskil L'David).

7. Joan Nathan, Jewish Cooking in America, (Alfred A. Knopf, Inc. 1994).

8. Rabbi I. Harold Sharfman, The First Rabbi (Malibu: Joseph Simon-Pangloss Press, 1988)

9. Ibid.

10. Ibid.

11. The Jewish-American History Documentation Foundation. http://www.jewish-history.com/civilwar/seder

12. Joan Nathan, Jewish Cooking in America, (Alfred A. Knopf, Inc. 1994).

13. Ibid.

14. Ibid.

15. Ibid.

16. Saul Bernstein, "The Beginnings of OU Kosher," http//www.oukosher.org

17. Kimberly Skopitz, "History of the Bagel," Page Wise, Inc. 2004

18. Joan Nathan, Jewish Cooking in America, (Alfred A. Knopf, Inc. 1994).

19. Ibid.

20. Ibid.

21. Margie Pensak, "You've Come a Long Way Star-K," 2004.

22. Jimmy Carter Library and Museum, "The Camp David Accords After Twenty-Five Years," http//www.jimmycarterlbrary.org/documents/campdavid25

23. Joy Katzen Guthrie, "A Thriving Jewish Life on the Northern Frontier," 2005. http//www.joyfulvoice.net/joyalaska

24. Marlene Adler Marks, "Lone Prarie," The Jewish Journal of Greater Los Angeles, April, 14 2000.

25. Joan Nathan, Jewish Cooking in America, (Alfred A. Knopf, Inc. 1994).

26. Aliza Karp, "Kosher Boy Scouts," Kashrus Magazine, June 2001

27. Rabbi Mitchell Ackerson, U.S. Army chaplain, senior rabbi Iraq combat theater. As told to the author by Rabbi Ackerson.

28. Israel News Agency. http//www.israelnewsagaency.com/israelastronautilanramon.

Numbers

customs for waiting between meat and milk, 37

Far East tuna production, 201–203

fats
from kosher animals, 36
from nonkosher sources, 189

federal regulation of milk, 32

fermented grain products. *See* kosher for Passover

fertilized eggs, 32

fins, 51-52

fire, as kashering agent, 156

fish
blood of, 31
"kosher shrimp," 44
meat and, 117
oils from, 188
production plant supervision, 199–203
scales of, 51-52, 63, 180

Fishbein, Susie, 119

Five Books of Moses. *See* Torah

flavorings, 189–190, 207–211

fleishig. *See* meat

foil, food wrapped in, 41

food as life. *See* holistic understanding of kosher; Whole Foods Market

food blessed by rabbis. *See* myths and facts of kashrus

food chemicals. *See* additives

food processors, 150, 157

food-related blessings. *See* blessings

forbidden foods. *See* entries at nonkosher

forbidden tree. *See* tree of knowledge

four-chambered stomachs of animals, 23–24, 26. *See also* kosher animals

fowl (birds), 36

fraud, 215

fresh fruit. See fruits

friends. *See* challenges to keeping kosher; Judaism, identity and awareness

fringe benefits of kosher food, 12, 14, 149

See also myths and facts of kashrus

fruit bowls, 148

fruits
agricultural-based commandments, 48–50
blessings over, 107
eaten cold, 70, 179
infestation of, 34, 117, 189, 204

frying pans, 152

G

Garden of Eden, 84–88

gelatin, 189

Gentiles
as consumers of kosher products, 81
kosher laws related to, 38–39, 45–46
mutual respect between friends, 75
social cohesiveness of Jews, 14, 38

George Foreman grills, 152

giraffes, 202

Girl Scout cookies, 197

glassware, 46, 148

glatt kosher, 33

goals, personal, 24, 102

goats in mother's milk, 173–174

God. *See also* Creation of the world; spirituality
blessings, as source of, 111–113
commitment to, 29–30
importance of kosher laws to, 182–184
partnership with man, 116–117
physical pleasures, as gifts from, 176–178
presence of, 94–95, 102–103, 145. *See also* blessings
relationship with Jewish nation, 85, 94
tests by, 26–30

"good" as kabbalistic insight, 88–91

"good *hechsherim*," 211–217. *See also* hechsherim

government regulation of milk, 32

grain products. *See also* bakeries; breads

ruminant animals, 23–24. *See also* kosher animals

S

salad bowls, plastic, 148
salads, recipes for, 125–129
salmon, 199–201, 203. *See also* fish
salting meat. *See* blood of kosher animals; kosher salt
sanctity. *See* holiness
sanitary foods. *See* cleanliness of kosher food
scales of fish, 51-52, 63, 180
self-cleaning ovens, 156, 160
self-control, 22–23, 70–71
separation level of *kedusha*, 101
separation of milk and meat. *See* milk and meat
serrated knives, 156
Seventh-Day Adventists, 81, 214
sexual relations, 96–98, 104
Shearith Israel, Congregation, 192, 193
Shechina. *See* presence of God
shechita. *See* slaughtering
shehakol blessing, 109, 117–118
shellfish, 51
shelves, storage, 148
Shir Ha'maalot, 112
shiviis, 50
shmittah, 50
shochet. *See* slaughtering
shopping for kosher food, 142, 167. *See also* grocery stores
silver, 151
silverware, 151, 156. *See also* utensils
Sinai (mountain), 93–94
sinks, 149, 157, 161
sixty-to-one ratio of milk to meat, 42
skin of fish, 180
slaughtering. *See also* blood of kosher animals; supervision of kosher food
    death of animals before, 36

giraffes, 202
glatt kosher, 33
imperfections in kosher animals, 28
kedusha (holiness) of, 96
knives for slaughtering, 36, 106
laws detailed in Talmud, 171–174
shechita, defined, 36
shochet, defined, 36
as tests by God, 27–28
small appliances, 157. *See also specific appliance by name*
soaking meat. *See* blood of kosher animals
social challenges. *See* challenges to keeping kosher
Song of Ascents, 112
soul, 83–118. *See also* spirituality
    body, fusion with. *See* holistic understanding of kosher
    body vs., 70–71, 86–88, 103
    creation of, by God, 13
    nonkosher food, effect on, 14, 23–27
    tree of knowledge and, 85–88, 90, 219
soups, recipes for, 122–124
spice racks, 148
Spinach Linguine with Walnut Cream Sauce, 134
spiritual growth, 98–104, 153–154, 187–188
spirituality. *See also* soul; tikkun
    body and soul, fusion of. *See* holistic understanding of kosher
    elevating food, 34
    Exodus from Egypt, purpose of, 166
    icons for (in this book), 17, 18
    kabbalistic insights into eating, 88–91
    kavanah, 92, 114–115
    kedushah, 93–98, 104
    laws as instructions for life, 47
    planting and building, 98–104
    potential for growth, 98–104
    promoting with kosher, 12–15, 19–24
    sensitivity to God's presence, 94–95, 103, 145. *See also* blessings

Meet Our Chefs

Susie Fishbein

The cooking world can be a bit elitist, and there are those who would look askance at pairing the words "elegant and gourmet" together with "kosher." Thanks to Susie Fishbein, that may never be the case again.

Susie Fishbein is a one-woman revolution. Her ground-breaking books have opened up a whole new world of possibilities to kosher cooks, chefs, and moms across the country and around the world.

Susie Fishbein is the author of the wildly successful cookbooks, *Kosher by Design*, *Kosher by Design Entertains*, and the newly released *Kosher by Design: Kids in the Kitchen*. She has spent most of 2005 on a tour traveling around the country and giving cooking demonstrations. She has appeared on *The Today Show* with Katie Couric, on *Allie & Jack*, on *Sheila Bridges Designer Living*, as well as on several network news show cooking segments. Additionally, she has taught at the prestigious De Gustibus Cooking School in New York.

Susie Fishbein is a mother of four children – three girls and a boy. A graduate of Queens College in New York, she taught fourth grade for several years at a progressive school in Oceanside, NY.

To order books by Susie Fishbein go to—
http://www.kosherbydesign.com.

Praise for *Kosher By Design*

"This is a cookbook that can compete with any fine cookbook on the market and would make a welcome gift to any kosher hostess."

Detroit Jewish News

"Fishbein has produced a volume that straddles that delicate line between modern and traditional and between refined cuisine and everyday ease."

Publishers Weekly

Scott Sunshine

Chef Scott Sunshine. . . in his own words:

"I love to cook. I started cooking when I was eight years old, and for as long as I can remember, I was always involved in helping my grandmother with holiday preparations in the kitchen. If it was Chanukah, I was helping with the potato latkes, and if it was a major occasion, like Sunday football on television, then I was helping make my father's favorite dish— chocolate-covered halvah followed by salami and eggs with beans.

For my Bar Mitzvah, I received a copy of the *Fanny Farmer Cookbook* which got me started experimenting with cooking. When I got to college, I went to work for the food service company and met a retired navy cook whom everyone called Cookie the Chef. It was at that time that I learned how to produce large quantities of food and also began to understand the fine art of seasoning food. Without a doubt, I was becoming a bona fide Foodie. I was soon reading several cooking magazines and cookbooks just for fun.

Before you could say *shwarma*, I was in Israel, and I ended up living there for seven years. It was there that I learned that the only limitation on great kosher food is one's imagination. I met Jews from dozens of countries, each had his or her own delicious cuisine, and every dish could be prepared kosher. While in Israel, I was a chef at a kosher restaurant at the Tel Aviv Hilton. Upon my return to the States, I worked for the New York Hilton where we served presidents, prime ministers, and plenty of regular folks too.

I have prepared food for as few as two people and as many as fifteen thousand. I am now semi-old, a "bit" overweight, and bald. I currently do restaurant consulting, as well as specialized catering at events such as The Super Bowl, The Masters and other PGA events, The Preakness, NASCAR, and the ESPN Great Outdoor Games. When I'm lucky, I get to do a little bit of cooking for the Apisdorf family, and when I'm really lucky, Shimon invites my sons and me over for his famous latkes, which is about all he knows how to cook.

If you are planning to have five thousand of your closest friends over for brunch, or even something more modest, please give me a call. I love to cook! You can reach me at (443) 929-1625 or shemesh511@comcast.net."

leviathan press

wisdom for the mind, inspiration for the soul™

EXPERIENCE THE HOLIDAYS WITH
SHIMON APISDORF

ROSH HASHANAH YOM KIPPUR SURVIVAL KIT

Shimon Apisdorf
Benjamin Franklin Award winner

There you are; it's the middle of High Holy Day services, and frankly, you're confused. Enter—the *Rosh Hashanah Yom Kippur Survival Kit*. This book follows the order of the services and masterfully blends wisdom, humor and down-to-earth spirituality. It's like having a knowledgeable friend sitting right next to you in synagogue.

"The Rosh Hashanah Yom Kippur Survival Kit is fun, meaningful and brilliantly written. If I had the resources, I would buy a copy for every Jew in America."

Rabbi Ephraim Z. Buchwald
Founder, National Jewish Outreach Program

THE SURVIVAL KIT FAMILY HAGGADAH

Shimon Apisdorf

The only Haggadah in the world featuring the Matzahbrei Family. A loveable family of matzah people that guide you and your family through a delightful, insightful, spiritual, and fun seder. Featuring the "talking Haggadah," and a revolutionary translation. Never again will you read a paragraph in the Haggadah and say, "Huh, what's that supposed to mean?"
This Haggadah is the perfect companion to *Judaism in a Nutshell: PASSOVER*.

"Valuable and entertaining. It will add to the significance and enjoyment of Passover in any Jewish home."

Michael Medved
Nationally syndicated radio talk show host,
best-selling author and veteran film critic

CHANUKAH: Eight Nights of Light, Eight Gifts for the Soul
Shimon Apisdorf
Benjamin Franklin Award winner

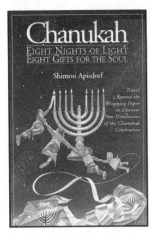

This book takes you way beyond the wrapping paper to discover a little known spiritual dimension of Chanukah. From the lighting of the candles to the dreidel to the Maccabees, this book explores fascinating dimensions of the Chanukah celebration. Includes everything a family needs to experience, enjoy, and be inspired by the holiday.

THE ONE HOUR PURIM PRIMER
Shimon Apisdorf

This book has everything a family needs to understand, celebrate, and enjoy Purim. User-friendly. Packed with great ideas for adults and children. Also includes a complete Hebrew-English Megillah/Book of Esther with brief explanations and commentary.

MORE FROM LEVIATHAN PRESS

THE DEATH OF CUPID: Reclaiming the Wisdom of Love, Dating, Romance and Marriage
Nachum Braverman & Shimon Apisdorf

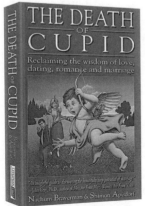

The Death of Cupid is divided into four sections: The Wisdom of Marriage, The Wisdom of Dating, The Wisdom of Sex, and The Wisdom of Romance. This book speaks equally to singles in search of love and to couples seeking to deepen their relationship.

"An insightful guide to discovering the beautifully deep potential of marriage."

John Gray, Ph.D.,
Author, *Men Are From Mars, Women Are From Venus*

REMEMBER MY SOUL:
What To Do In Memory Of A Loved One
Lori Palatnik

An informative, insightful, and practical guide to the Jewish understanding of death and mourning. The book includes a guided journey through *shiva* and the stages of Jewish mourning. While reading the book, readers also create a *Diary of Remembrance* that becomes a personal keepsake.

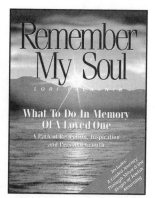

"Remember My Soul teaches the bereaved to harness the rich resources of Jewish spirituality. It demonstrates how to turn the pain of losing a dear one into a vehicle for human wholeness."

Rabbi E.B. Freedman
Director of Jewish Hospice Services, Hospice of Michigan

THE BIBLE FOR THE CLUELESS BUT CURIOUS
Nachum Braverman
Benjamin Franklin Award Winner

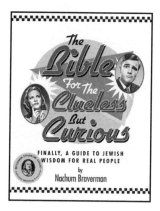

This is the award-winning book that launched the *Clueless but Curious* series. Maybe the last time you read the Bible was in Sunday School, or maybe you never read it at all. *The Bible for the Clueless but Curious* won't throw a bunch of "thous" and "forsooths" at you and won't try to make you feel guilty about anything. This book is for thoughtful people who have never had a chance to discover the world of wisdom in the Bible and see how it can actually be relevant to life in the 21st century. A cast of fun and friendly icons help make this book a delightful read.

"Nachum Braverman is one of the most provocative and inspiring teachers in the Jewish world today."

David Wilstein
Past General Chairman United Jewish Fund of Los Angeles
President, Realtech Leasing and Management

THE JUDAISM IN A NUTSHELL COLLECTION

For people who are long on curiosity, but short on time. This unique series of books now includes four great titles:

Judaism in a Nutshell: God

Judaism in a Nutshell: Holidays

Judaism in a Nutshell: Israel

Judaism in a Nutshell: Passover

Each one of these books presents just about everything you need to know about one of the pillars of Judaism.

"Israel is the most powerful and the most volatile issue Jewish students confront on campus. This book will shed light on the most confusing issues surrounding Israel and also give students a more profound understanding of what it means to have a Jewish homeland."

Avi Weinstein
Director, Hillel's Joseph Meyerhoff Center
for Jewish Learning

""The ideas are very deep, yet the style is a delight and easy to read. It would be a good idea to reread this book every few years—it's just that important."

Andrew Goldfinger, Ph.D,
Assistant Director of the Space Department's
Mission Concept and Analysis Group,
Author, *Thinking About Creation*

ZAP! POW! BAM! Comic Book Superheroes and the Jewish Mind
Simcha Weinstein

A fascinating look at the uncanny relationship between Jewish thought, culture, history, and many of your favorite heroes. Batman, Superman and many, many more.

AT RISK BUT NOT BEYOND REACH: A Real World Guide to Understanding and Nurturing the Teenagers You Love
Rabbi Daniel Schonbuch

Teenagers are mystifying, lovable, and often terrifying. For parents and educators who are struggling to raise, nurture, teach or guide a teenager, this book is a must. Presents a thoughtful, practical, tested, and easy to implement strategy.

CHEAT SHEETS

There are times when you need information that is succinct, without frills, and highly informative. This is where Cheat Sheets come in. Each Cheat Sheet is "just" an 8.5 x 14 brochure, yet each contains so much information you will think you just read a book. After all, isn't that what cheat sheets are all about?

MY HIGH HOLIDAY CHEAT SHEET	FALL 2005
MY HANNUKAH CHEAT SHEET	WINTER 2005
MY PURIM CHEAT SHEET	SPRING 2006
MY PASSOVER CHEAT SHEET	SPRING 2006
MY ISRAEL CHEAT SHEET	COMING SOON
MY JEWISH HISTORY CHEAT SHEET	ON THE HORIZON
MY SHAVUOT CHEAT SHEET	BEFORE YOU KNOW IT
MY SUKKOT CHEAT SHEET	JUST AROUND THE CORNER
MY TEN COMMANDMENTS CHEAT SHEET	TOP SECRET
THE CHEAT SHEETS FOR TEENS SERIES	NOT TELLING

LEVIATHAN PRESS ORDER INFORMATION

To Order:
Phone: 1-800-LEVIATHAN (538-4284) or (410) 653-0300
Email: orders@leviathanpress.com
Online: www.leviathanpress.com
www.jewishcheatsheets.com

NON-PROFIT BULK ORDERS

All of our products can be purchased at significant bulk order discounts by schools, synagogues, educational institutions, and other non-profit organizations. Cheat Sheets and many of our books can be customized to promote your organization.

For special prices and customization options:
Call: 1-800-LEVIATHAN (538-4284) or (410) 653-0300
Email: info@leviathanpress.com

BOOKS BY SUSIE FISHBEIN

KOSHER BY DESIGN
KOSHER BY DESIGN ENTERTAINS
KOSHER BY DESIGN KIDS IN THE KITCHEN

These three books include hundreds of great recipes and page after page of dazzling full color photos. Also included are dozens of menu suggestions, easy-to-follow instructions, and tips on food preparation and table décor.

The *Kosher By Design* cookbook series. Order now from www.kosherbydesign.com or call 1-800-MESORAH (637-6724)—and save 10% off the list price PLUS FREE SHIPPING (free ground shipping in the continental USA). In order to receive this special FREE SHIPPING offer, you must enter promotion code "KOSHERSHIP" on the payment screen when you check out.

And God created the giant sea creatures …

Genesis 1:21

These sea creatures were the Leviathan. One male and one female. Had they been allowed to mate, they would have destroyed the world…At the end of history, God will make a meal for the righteous from the flesh of the Leviathan.

Talmud

The Leviathan represents something of 'giant' spiritual potential.

Maharal of Prague

The Leviathan is a mystical, aquatic creature linked to a realm of deep spiritual insight.
The Leviathan evokes the search for timeless ideas as relevant today as they were eons ago.
Since 1992, Leviathan Press has brought rays of Jewish wisdom and spirituality to the English–speaking public.

 leviathan press™

wisdom for the mind, inspiration for the soul™

www.leviathanpress.com

About the Author

Shimon Apisdorf is an award-winning author whose books have been read by hundreds of thousands of people all over the world. Shimon has gained a worldwide reputation for his ability to extract the essence of classical Jewish wisdom and show how it can be relevant to the essential issues facing the mind, heart, and soul in today's world. His writings speak poignantly, with rare sensitivity and with humor, to people of all backgrounds. Shimon grew up in Cleveland, Ohio and attended the University of Cincinnati, Telshe Yeshiva, and Yeshivat Aish HaTorah in Jerusalem where he received rabbinic ordination. He currently resides with his wife Miriam and their children in Baltimore. Shimon and Miriam can be spotted taking long walks along the Inner Harbor. The Apisdorf family can be found at Orioles games, on roller coasters, and at Melava Malkas on Saturday nights. As for the Ravens—anything is better than the Steelers! You can reach Shimon at— shimon@leviathanpress.com.

Special Thanks: Star-K
I want to express my gratitude to the Star-K of Baltimore. Their vision, commitment, and generous grant to the Jewish Literacy Foundation made this book possible. The entire Star-K staff was always ready to help in any way they could. Particular thanks go to Dr. Avrom Pollak and Mrs. Margie Pensak. Rabbi Moshe Heinemann devoted hours to preparation of the manuscript. The opportunity to spend time with a scholar like Rabbi Heinemann was an experience I will cherish for years to come.
Thank you Star-K.

Special Thanks: Jewish Literacy Foundation
Rabbi Yigal Segal of the Jewish Literacy Foundation was the first to conceive of this book. It was his dedication to the highest ideals of Jewish education that ensured that what was a great idea became, what I hope, is a good book.
Thank you JLF.